Praise for *Unprepared to Entrepreneur*

'Frank, solidly researched and packed with fascinating insights about the reality of building a career around your personal brand – this is the sort of book I wish had been around when I started my career. Sonya Barlow is an exciting voice shaking up the world of entrepreneurship and telling it like it is.' ANDREA THOMPSON, EDITOR-IN-CHIEF, *MARIE CLAIRE*

'An informative guide for anyone looking to become an entrepreneur. Setting off on your entrepreneurial journey can be daunting, but Sonya Barlow breaks everything down clearly to help you on your way to success.' ANNA JONES AND DEBBIE WOSSKOW OBE, CO-FOUNDERS, ALLBRIGHT

'The book every entrepreneur needs. Reading through this toolkit, it had everything included that would make you feel inspired, prepared and ready to tackle the business world. *Unprepared to Entrepreneur* truly is a must-read with so many real stories from real people. Sonya Barlow has really hit the nail on the head here.' ANNA FLOCKETT, CEO, *STARTUPS* MAGAZINE

'*Unprepared to Entrepreneur* is a book for any entrepreneur that has a side hustle or passion project and wants to take it to the next level. Not only does it give advice and simple exercises to build their business, but it also provides a truthful glimpse into what being an entrepreneur is.' CHARLOTTE WILLIAMS, FOUNDER, SEVENSIX AGENCY

'An honest and real approach to entrepreneurship. I am an entrepreneur myself and have loved reading her journey and can resonate with her experiences. As a South Asian woman I was glad to read the story about a great South Asian entrepreneur that hasn't let setbacks make her quit. A fantastic read for anyone looking to join the entrepreneurial journey.' EBBA QURESHI, FOUNDER AND CEO, FEMGAMES

'This is a very personal journey and Sonya Barlow's route to success is full of useful advice. Her voice is clear and her understanding of the modern business environment is insightful. She may not have learnt how to complete a tax return at her business school but she has learnt to research, to write and to reflect. This is a fascinating book and invaluable to anyone thinking of starting their own business today.' IAN DANIEL, BUSINESS AND MANAGEMENT LECTURER, BAYES BUSINESS SCHOOL

'*Unprepared to Entrepreneur* is the real deal, filled with hard-earned lessons, practical advice and relatable stories from Sonya Barlow's professional journey. It's inspirational, but also brings entrepreneurship down to earth: this book reminds us that it isn't reserved for a rare few, but a path any of us can follow.' KATIE CARROLL, HEAD OF NEWS, NORTH AMERICA AND UK, LINKEDIN

'What an inspirational and useful toolkit. I work with small business owners daily who would really benefit from reading this book. I will be recommending it to all my contacts!' LAUREN MALONE, HEAD OF FEMALE ENTREPRENEURSHIP, ENTERPRISE NATION

'Sonya Barlow provides us with a great combination of her own experience and practical guidance for aspiring entrepreneurs who would like to follow her lead. She has a wonderful insight into the sorts of hurdles that entrepreneurs encounter and the best ways to surmount them.' MARTIN RICH, SENIOR LECTURER, BAYES BUSINESS SCHOOL

'As a slightly unmanageable, self-made entrepreneur – with fingers in many pies – I found this book very reassuring, with its relatable anecdotes and optimistic approach. Sonya Barlow's accessibility, inclusivity and refreshing innovation makes me certain that any starting entrepreneur should own a copy.' MIKA SIMMONS, ACTRESS, FILMMAKER AND HOST OF THE HAPPY VAGINA PODCAST

'*Unprepared to Entrepreneur* is the perfect toolkit for recent graduates and aspiring entrepreneurs. It is jam-packed with great advice, practical steps you can take and diverse case studies which challenge the idea of entrepreneurs as big, successful, tech innovators.' OLIVIA HANLON, FOUNDER AND CEO, GIRLS IN MARKETING

'A delightful read, full of experiences and advice for those who want to get out of their comfort zone and understand the journey of being unprepared to be an entrepreneur. It paints a clear picture that you don't need to be rich or prepared to start something; it's all within you and the way you react to surroundings.' RITESH JAIN, CO-FOUNDER, INFYNIT

'Sonya Barlow is an impressive entrepreneur who offers valuable advice on how to overcome the failures and the doubts that many founders have to take an idea and turn it into a successful business. There is more to be learned from leaders like Barlow who have the ability to transform adversity into an opportunity to help other entrepreneurs.' RUSS SHAW CBE, FOUNDER, TECH LONDON ADVOCATES AND GLOBAL TECH ADVOCATES

'An entrepreneurship book packed with honest reflection, refreshing ideas and truly inspiring stories about success and failure. I recommend it to students, educators and professionals who are eager to learn more about the – sometimes not-so-glamorous – reality of starting a business.' SABRINA VIETH, PRINCIPAL LECTURER IN ENTREPRENEURSHIP AND INNOVATION, COVENTRY UNIVERSITY

'Sonya Barlow's journey helps her bring to life some vital lessons for any budding entrepreneur. The case studies add further lessons and validation of key points. The reflection areas help entrepreneurs think about how they might put lessons learned into practice. A mini MBA.' DR SANDEEP BANSAL, INNOVATION FACULTY, HARVARD MEDICAL SCHOOL AND FOUNDER, MEDIA CREATIONS

'For many people, the adventures of self-employment and entrepreneurship never begin because they don't know where to start. This is especially true for potential founders who are hindered by their social background, the inherent injustice of today's economic system, or simply the daily grind of earning a living instead of following your dreams. Sonya Barlow specializes in helping someone like that – maybe someone like you? – to help them make it anyway.' SEBASTIAN ESSER, CO-FOUNDER, STEADY

'In these turbulent times it's so important to forge your own path. Sonya Barlow has done just that and her book is a great combination of advice, life stories and practical steps anyone can take to bring their idea to life. Happy reading and good luck!' TABITHA GOLDSTAUB, FOUNDER, COGX AND CHAIR OF THE UK GOVERNMENT'S AI COUNCIL

'A must-read book on the realities of entrepreneurship. One I wish had existed before I took the plunge. Anyone reading this will be a better founder and operator because of it.' TOM MCGILLYCUDDY, TICKR

'This book is a must-read for every budding entrepreneur. Not only does it provide sound advice, but it also covers the journeys of so many others that changed careers to become entrepreneurs.' VANESSA VALLELY, FOUNDER, WEARETHECITY

'I wish I had had this book when I started my business. The inspiring stories of challenges, hurdles and failures will resonate with many, especially with aspiring entrepreneurs from diverse backgrounds, who will identify with Sonya Barlow's story and will now have practical advice to rely on.' ZAHRA KHAN, FOUNDER, FEYA CAFÉ

Unprepared to Entrepreneur

A method to the madness of starting your own business

Sonya Barlow

KoganPage

First published in Great Britain and the United States in 2021 by Kogan Page Limited

2nd Floor, 45 Gee Street
London
EC1V 3RS
United Kingdom
www.koganpage.com

122 W 27th St, 10th Floor
New York, NY 10001
USA

4737/23 Ansari Road
Daryaganj
New Delhi 110002
India

Kogan Page books are printed on paper from sustainable forests.

ISBNs

Harback   978 1 3986 0148 2
Paperback   978 1 3986 0146 8
Ebook   978 1 3986 0147 5

British Library Cataloguing-in-Publication Data

A CIP record for this book is available from the British Library.

Library of Congress Cataloging-in-Publication Data

Names: Barlow, Sonya, author.
Title: Unprepared to entrepreneur: a method to the madness of starting your own business / Sonya Barlow.
Description: London; New York, NY: Kogan Page, 2021. | Includes bibliographical references and index.
Identifiers: LCCN 2021031398 (print) | LCCN 2021031399 (ebook) | ISBN 9781398601468 (paperback) | ISBN 9781398601482 (hardback) | ISBN 9781398601475 (ebook)
Subjects: LCSH: New business enterprises. | Business planning. | Entrepreneurship.
Classification: LCC HD62.5 .B3635 2021 (print) | LCC HD62.5 (ebook) | DDC 658.1/1–dc23
LC record available at https://lccn.loc.gov/2021031398
LC ebook record available at https://lccn.loc.gov/2021031399

Typeset by Integra Software Services, Pondicherry
Print production managed by Jellyfish
Printed and bound by CPI Group (UK) Ltd, Croydon, CR0 4YY

Contents

About the author

Sonya Barlow is an award-winning entrepreneur, the founder of the @LMFnetwork, a diversity business coach and a motivational speaker. Her efforts are focused on bridging the skills gap and creating inclusive cultures. She has delivered two TEDx talks and is an international keynote speaker. Sonya has had her articles published in *Metro* newspaper, *Sifted EU* and *The Telegraph*. Her businesses have partnered with global companies including Babbel, Steady, Institute of Coding, GoCo Group, Barclays, the *Financial Times* and BMW. In 2020, she was named as one of the Most Influential Women in Tech (*Computer Weekly*), Winner of the Women in Software Changemakers (Makers and Google), Top 50 BAME Entrepreneurs (*TechRound*) and Future Shaper 2020 (*Marie Claire*). In 2021, Sonya was shortlisted as a runner up for *Forbes 30 Under 30*, recognized as a LinkedIn Changemaker for gender equality and asked to present BBC Asian Network's *The Everyday Hustle*, which is a show about getting started, getting ahead and getting rich from a career or business. Identifying as a first-generation immigrant, Sonya has proudly carried her South Asian heritage and advocated the social stigmas faced by under-represented intersectional communities, especially ethnic minorities and women. Having been raised in an average working-class family, she understands the importance of leading as a successful role model to encourage inclusion and has stapled this to the forefront of all her business collaborations. Sonya can be found on LinkedIn (www.linkedin.com/in/sonyabarlow) and Instagram (@Sonyabarlowuk).

Foreword

I have a dream. I dream of a future where no woman waits to start a business. I dream of a future where every woman has conquered her fear of failure, and has found the courage to embrace the unknown.

I dream of a future where our success is not defined by the status society grants us, but by our individual capacity to design a life based on our values and priorities.

Fortunately, many of us women today are already building our dream careers thanks to the efforts of entrepreneurship and I am so grateful to be in this group of brave souls. But it took a long time for me to get here, and I must confess I'm still on this journey of self-fulfilment through entrepreneurship.

As soon as I started working, I knew I wanted to be my own boss. My first steady job was working in a call centre during the first summer vacation of university. The repetitive nature of the job, reading a script off a screen, made me yearn for more inter-action. Moving into a retail role I loved the thrill of sales, but still felt something was missing. When I finally landed a job in a tech startup after graduation I felt at home at work for the first time in my life. But that feeling didn't last; I soon realized the tech industry had a serious diversity and inclusion problem.

Despite working my ass off and smashing my goals, I saw peers who looked more like leadership than me, promoted quicker than me, and receiving bigger pay rises than me. This wasn't about performance any more, this was about bias and the failure to acknowledge it and address it.

I knew I wanted to do something about this – but how? Could there be a business in this? I had no idea how to find out the answers to my most burning questions, and I had no idea how to start. By stumbling, failing and falling and learning to love taking risks, I found myself a founder of Hustle Crew, a diversity company on a mission to make tech more inclusive.

Five years into the journey, I'm running one of the most established diversity-in-tech communities in the world.

If only a book like this had existed when I first started: a manual to show me the ropes, help me overcome challenges and most of all give me the confidence boost to keep going, even when I didn't have the answers.

I've known Sonya for years now, since Like Minded Females first appeared on my radar through LinkedIn. She exemplifies so many of the ideal characteristics of an exceptional entrepreneur: a relentless drive, an authentic vulnerability and a commitment to always acting in line with her values, passions and beliefs.

Sonya's work is about ensuring women and marginalized groups across the world succeed as much as her own personal journey of fulfilment. In this book she reflects on the ups and downs, the lessons learned, and the unique challenges women, especially women of colour, face as we navigate the rapidly changing landscape of entrepreneurship.

Take heart in knowing investing in this book is investing in yourself, in your personal and professional development and of course – in your business! Embrace the journey, for all its pain and glory, and know that the words contained here will give you confidence and comfort whenever you need it.

Happy reading!

Abadesi Osunsade
Founder and CEO of Hustle Crew,
a diversity-in-tech community and training company,
and co-host of the weekly podcast Techish

Acknowledgements

Thank you to my family, who have always supported my ambitions, no matter how wild they may seem, raised me to have an opinion and encouraged me to give everything a try. My friends, for reading through my notes, picking up my calls and reassuring me when I didn't know what to write. And to my partner: from reading early drafts to staying patient through the long nights and bringing me countless chais, he is the co-author without the credit. This book is for anyone who wants to bet on themselves and their business idea but is told no, doesn't know where to begin, or doesn't have the self-belief.

CHAPTER ONE

Are you prepared to be an entrepreneur?

It was spring 2018, and I was on my way to brunch at one of my favourite venues opposite London Bridge station. I had already planned my meal – smashed avocado on toast, hot chai latte with extra cinnamon and a tall glass of fresh orange juice. This wasn't just any brunch, but the first event I had organized as part of my plan to create a community.

The night before, I had laid out my best outfit on the dressing table. I woke up with butterflies like it was my first day of school. I arrived 30 minutes early, sat on every seat to determine which was right for me, then proceeded to order. This was going to be a momentous occasion, so I took out my iPhone and started taking pictures of the venue and the other diners. I wanted to capture this moment as a part of my story – big things were about to happen.

Forty-five minutes later, the waitress kindly asked for the table back and brought over the bill.

After three weeks of planning and 12 reservations, the soft launch was a complete failure. That was my first experience of launching a business, a community, a brand.

Welcome to entrepreneurship

I had 12 reservations confirmed via email, which turned into 12 no-shows. I was disappointed – little did I know that this underwhelming lack of an event would change my life forever.

Entrepreneurship is life-changing. You are taking a risk on an idea and yourself. If that idea fails, it can be crushing, but the notion of not pursuing that idea can feel way worse. It's difficult to define the limits of entrepreneurship as the possibilities are endless. Letting go of your own reservations and actually starting are often the hardest part.

Stepping into the world of entrepreneurship feels like the first day of secondary school. Everything feels new, everyone seems bigger and more experienced. Starting a business, building a brand, even writing this book takes a lot of hard work and determination. You sit down, ready to put pen to paper, secretly hoping that a flow of ideas will start hitting the page. It's your business, your vision, your future, and the idea is so clear in your mind, so why is it that as soon as you go to write it down, you draw a blank? If, like me, you have been in this situation multiple times before, then don't worry. This is common and you will overcome it.

This book will take you on a journey on how to discover your business and brand, and provide you with all the tools you need to become your own boss! Are you ready?

How to make the most of this book

Don't read this book all at once. It's imperative that you take time to reflect on each chapter and story. Truthfully, I don't understand the habit of reading self-help or business books in one go, especially when many require mental effort and take you on a journey of self-realization. There is no rush. Starting a business is a marathon, not a sprint. Take your time, ask questions and enjoy the process. I have included a workbook section at the end of each chapter for you to use for notes or to mind map. This is all work in progress and no thought should be left unwritten.

Becoming an accidental entrepreneur

Entrepreneurship is one cup madness, one cup dedication and three cups of strategically winging it until something satisfactory is made.

I can't help but laugh to myself that I've written an entrepreneurship book. My idea wasn't necessarily a business idea to start with; I never intended to become an entrepreneur. I just had an idea to try to get me out of my own 'grey area', which is an expression that I use to describe a feeling of dissatisfaction with something, or a frustration that one hasn't found a solution for (yet). In fact, this bad place or grey area was the perfect place for me to start an entrepreneurial journey. As you will see throughout this book, it is also something that other award-winning entrepreneurs have recognized in their own journey.

A bad place makes for a great story

I was a lonely and stressed young professional climbing the corporate ladder only to have it pulled from underneath me every time I climbed a step too high. I felt no community around me, struggled to name close colleagues or allies, and had nowhere to turn when wanting to discuss progress, pay and challenging work scenarios. I felt alone and isolated, despite being globally connected and living in London.

Becoming an entrepreneur wasn't something I had planned, which is often the case for many business owners. I was an accidental entrepreneur and unprepared for what this new world would ask of me. Within 18 months, I went from being unhappy and unfulfilled working in the technology industry, to winning awards for my business idea, starting a second business, impacting the lives of people globally, failing fast, finding gratitude in every moment and writing this book. It wasn't always easy.

With no real starting plan, I began following a few basic and fundamental steps that required me to create, test and launch my business idea.

Contrary to what you're taught through institutionalized education, a business plan is not the first thing you create when becoming an entrepreneur. In my opinion, the idea that you must have a formalized business plan in order to even start a business is outdated and unrealistic. Having to curate an intricate plan that is foolproof means that you are committed to a script for your business, thus often acting as a deterrent to you even getting started. As amazing as my journey sounds, I can't help but still feel like I am on a loop within a video game; running through fire, jumping through hoops and catching gold coins only to realize there is another level that is much more challenging. But only through having started can I progress and adapt to what the world throws at me.

In March 2020, we saw the world go into lockdown. The COVID-19 crisis meant job losses and a looming recession. During this time, I had hundreds of messages every week asking how I had started my business and if I could share my business plan and support people with their own entrepreneurial journeys. With job security at its lowest and many members of the public finding themselves in their own grey areas, it was inevitable that people would start exploring other ideas outside of the standard nine to five and this was one of the reasons I wanted to write this book.

If the global COVID-19 pandemic has taught us anything, it's that life is ever-changing. The same companies that weren't able to provide remote access before had to shift 100 per cent of their offerings; universities were forced to deliver their lessons online and we realized that digital connectivity was fundamental to staying afloat; the real winners of this new world were Zoom, Microsoft Teams and Google Hangouts, to name but a few. A bulletproof business plan doesn't save you from disruption. Getting yourself out there and being able to adapt are what will propel your businesses forward. Read on to learn how to prepare for launching your adaptable business.

Why must one prepare to be an entrepreneur?

Starting a business *will* shock your system. There is no such thing as a perfect plan or the *best* time to start. If you keep waiting, the *right* time will never come.

Start by focusing on the golden circle (Sinek, 2021) of 'what, how and why'. What do we do? How are we different? Why are we doing what we are doing? For many, the 'why' is the most important part of the circle as it confirms your business ethos and overall objective. According to more traditional ways of marketing, businesses that have a solid golden circle wouldn't need to adapt to the market as their objective and reasonings are sound and stable.

Fast-forward to 2021, this certainly isn't the case any more. Companies such as Apple and Uber have had to constantly evolve their business objectives, just to keep up with consumer needs and societal requirements. This type of innovation is what makes these companies stay afloat but this isn't to say that these types of business don't slip up from time to time.

When Apple launched in the 1970s, their main objective (or their why) focused on changing the way people viewed computers and wanted the technology industry to be more inclusive in terms of who could access the equipment. Despite their objective leading them to global success, a failure of theirs can be seen in the launch of the Apple Watch in 2015. According to *The Verge* (Duhaime-Ross, 2014), the initial Apple Watch prototype featured fitness tracking, health-oriented capabilities and wireless telecommunication but not a period tracker. This was rectified in 2019 when Apple released the upgraded version of the watch, but since period trackers had been around since 2013, this could be seen as a non-inclusive oversight that goes against their initial business plan objective.

In an interview with *Womanthology* (2017), Canva's founder Melanie Perkins shared that her initial business plan was to build a design toolkit that students could use without having to spend money on expensive design software. She mentions that because of her lack of experience, she was rejected by a number of investors before one decided to invest. If she had stopped after that first knockback, then Canva would not be the tool it is today.

These stories present a clear problem that the founders were aiming to solve. In each, it took hard work, many attempts and some failure along the way to become the business and brand that we all know today. What is the learning from this? It's okay if you don't know exactly what you're doing, it's completely fine to fail and face rejection, as long as you learn and are ready to change tack along the way.

Within the media, stories of wealthy and privileged founders are usually showcased. You read about the glamour of being your own boss, but you rarely read about how hard it is. There are very few stories narrating accessibility, business failures and real entrepreneurial challenges such as learning to say no, money management, how to prioritize your well-being and conquering your own procrastination. I am an ordinary person who has been able to build a successful business. However, despite attending business school and watching the likes of *Dragons' Den* on the television, it wasn't until I faced my own problems that I was able to find my feet in the world of entrepreneurship. This book is meant to share my journey and help others in similar situations.

Failures and grey areas: if the demand is there, what is holding you back?

Data tells us that entrepreneurship is on the rise

According to *SmallBizGenius* (Simovic, 2021), there are an estimated 582 million entrepreneurs globally and 31 million exist within the United States (Lange *et al*, 2019). In the UK, research by the FSB estimated that 5.7 million people considered themselves business owners, of which 99 per cent ticked the 'small or solo business' box when answering their survey (FSB, 2021). Additionally, as a result of the COVID-19 pandemic, SME loans found that 64 per cent of UK residents wanted to start their own business (Rosling, 2020) and the Allbright shared that three in four women wanted to set up their own business (Carrick, 2020). Small businesses, new businesses and entrepreneurs can generate around £1.9 trillion a year into the economy (IW Capital, 2019).

The truth is that 60 per cent of businesses fail within the first three years, according to research by DC Incubator (2019). Personally, I am a big fan of failure. For me, failure is merely being temporarily disrupted and having to find a new path to achieve the same or a similar goal. However, I believe that if we heard and understood the real stories of founders, the real challenges of business owners, and laid out how to solve these using digital media and communication, we'd all be able to have a clear understanding of how to run a successful business. Imagine it's a Friday night and you are heading out for dinner. If your friend texted you about the road being blocked or the train being delayed before you left the house, you would find an alternative route. That heads-up is this book. I am preparing you for entrepreneurship by reliving my own experiences, and I'm bringing fellow entrepreneurs along for the ride.

When first starting out, I found myself spending more time questioning my own ability, rather than focusing on what unique qualities I was bringing to the business.

The aftermath of the initial COVID-19 scare rewired my sense of entrepreneurship, purpose and measures of success. I began 2020 building myself up to boss status, only to lose 75 per cent of my income overnight. By April (after days of not being able to get out of bed, which is discussed in Chapter 8), I thought 'ah well – WHAT IF?' What if – I tried?

What if – I messaged this person?
What if – I changed my business model to align to my values?
What if – I focused on building my social presence from scratch?
What if – I started charging for my services?
What if – I took a moment out to enjoy the sunshine?
What if – I wrote a book that shares the stories of ordinary people doing extraordinary things?

There is no right or wrong way to start a business, to become a founder, to title yourself as an entrepreneur. Each and every leader I have interviewed for this book has spoken with such electricity. It's an instant burst of energy filled with compassion, community and commitment.

The greyer the area, the simpler the solution

Have you ever walked away from a conversation expecting at least a thank you? It's normal to think that a good job deserves a little praise. In 2018, I left a long-term position and was on to my second-ever corporate job. It felt great to have been offered a new role and even negotiated a higher salary (more on negotiation skills in Chapter 10). Leaving my current employer felt bitter-sweet. On my final day at the office, I walked in expecting a card or at least a heartfelt goodbye. It had been the case for many colleagues before – everyone would sign the obligatory goodbye card, then the team would go for the goodbye lunch and would politely wave the member of staff off at the end of the working day. It was basically an office tradition.

Instead, I spent lunchtime alone with a spicy wasabi soup. Apparently, my managers had forgotten to notify the wider team to say I was leaving. As if that wasn't bad enough, they decided to take a working from home day on my final day – despite asking me to come in and be office-based. Honestly, by 2 pm I was mentally over the whole experience. I walked into HR's office in my three-inch-heeled boots, handed in my laptop and under my breath said 'adios amigos'. That power walk alone made me feel like I had grown from graduate to corporate worker.

As I walked from the office to Hammersmith tube station, which felt like hours (in reality, it was about 10 minutes), a feeling of sadness, guilt and loneliness started to come over me.

I had worked there for two years and considered myself a part of the community. And yet, I walked out alone and frustrated. I looked around to see the world rushing past me. Being in London, everyone is always running from one place to another.

I felt alone and lost. That was my grey area. I had no purpose and so started planning my new identity as I had convinced myself that the current one wasn't good enough.

Who are you?

How do you feel about yourself? How would you describe yourself to a stranger?

Having a sense of belonging and identity are core to becoming a great entrepreneur. People will lean on you for advice and direction. In business, identity is important as it's the first element that speaks to potential customers and consumers. In an article published on *Thrive Global* (2018), writer Dina Marais, Business & Life Reinvention Coach, discusses identity as how we see ourselves, and the most important factor between success and failure. 'The sum of your thoughts and beliefs about your-self... your identity will determine how you show up in your business or job and life... It will reveal itself in your sales conversations, how you ask for money, how you make yourself visible.'

Working on your business is the same as working on yourself as an entrepreneur – you must allow yourself and the business to evolve in order to achieve your version of success for both.

Having a sense of identity gives you clear values to follow, core principles that direct your gut decisions and, most importantly, a reason for your actions or approach.

Being a yes girl in my first year of business made me lose focus. I had to remind myself that I was a business owner who could lose out on bids, projects and services for not being authentic.

What is this madness you've started?

Since graduating in 2015, I have entered four different work-spaces, each one smaller than the one before – which meant more work, more hats, more responsibilities. Between my first and second corporate roles I felt lost and insecure. I started the new role feeling out of my depth and unsure who to lean on. I walked in with a fresh mindset but hesitated in getting too close to my colleagues, in case there happened to be a repeat of the last time. My journey to work and back each day took 90 minutes, which gave me three hours of extra thinking time.

On one of these occasions, as I sat on the train from Paddington to Langley, I scrolled through my WhatsApp chats. They were limited and dry. Most of my friends were the ones I had met during my year abroad, who now lived in other continents. I decided to message a close university friend of mine to check in. We hadn't spoken for a couple of years but our friendship was such that it didn't matter. I mentioned my new conundrum and we ended up chatting and planned to meet up. At the same time,

I started to search for 'London-based networking events' and sent them her way, asking if she would be able to accompany me for moral support.

It was spring 2018 when we decided to attend our first networking event and it blew my mind. In the networking rooms, canapes were being served, the conversation was progressive and there were a lot of established businesswomen in attendance. As the evening ended, I exchanged notes with my friend and we both agreed this had been a success. This particular club had art on the walls, restrooms with towels instead of tissues and the fresh smell of books in its library.

I was sold into this life. This lifestyle. I wanted in.

Though I knew there was a cost of entry, I didn't think that the price would be the main discourager. Turns out, to find a sense of belonging and community, I was required to pay £1,500 per month excluding events, activities and tea. I giggled with embarrassment, held on tight to my chipped Barclaycard and walked out. I couldn't understand why we would be asked to pay nearly half the monthly cost of living in London (Numbeo, nd) just to meet like-minded people who wanted to succeed, when surely that should just happen naturally.

Was I that desperate for identity, friends and community?

Over a short period of time, the following emotions led me to become who I am today:

1 shock;
2 anger;
3 determination.

If I can't find a community, maybe they can't find me?!

This was both a question and a statement. That is *literally* where my life changed.

I don't know what it was or why it happened, but in that moment I felt this spark of energy and heard a voice that said 'What's the worst that can happen?'

Believing that I couldn't feel worse, I decided to go and find my own community. That was the beginning of the end of corporate life and the start of my entrepreneurial journey. Only, I didn't know that then.

The moment I exited from that overpriced networking club, I reactivated my LinkedIn account and founded what is now the LMF Network. The following nine things happened rapidly over the next two weeks.

I proceeded to:

1 create a closed 'women in career' LinkedIn group;
2 post information on careers, news and business tips;
3 design our first networking brunch event in London (because who doesn't love avocado on toast?);
4 share the networking event on LinkedIn and Eventbrite;
5 receive 12 confirmations from attendees for my first brunch;
6 convince myself we'd made it and launched this amazing network club;
7 fall from grace, when the restaurant asked for its table back 45 minutes after the booking time because no one showed up;
8 order three hot drinks, two large breakfasts and cry for 30 minutes;
9 be too ashamed to admit no one had showed up, so I announced on LinkedIn that seven people had.

After the initial failure of finding the community I longed for, I tried again. That also failed. It took three attempts to finally have one person attend a brunch. That one person was all it took – that one person gave me the reassurance that I was on to something, that my grey area was a similar shade to others' and we needed to bring some colour into our lives.

Slowly but surely, the community started to connect online and meet offline. We transitioned from summer brunches to winter socials. We took our LinkedIn content to Instagram and built a website. The whole movement was quickly picked up by companies that were eager to build community forums and individuals wanting to meet other people to discuss career, confidence and capabilities. Efforts to find out more turned into opportunities to speak, share and shout about our story. The story captured hearts and built the community. The business transitioned from a passion project to a limited company and soon ended up as a not-for-profit organization. The mission was, is and will continue to be to reduce inequalities, build confidence and accelerate careers.

And here we are. Here's us looping back to how it all began. I didn't go out searching for a business or wanting to build my brand, and never considered becoming my own boss.

I felt like an accidental entrepreneur. I have to admit that sometimes I still get this feeling but now I know much of this is imposter syndrome. The mixed feelings of accomplishment and fraud-like behaviour – I know I deserve to be here, but sometimes I can't help but compare myself with others.

Though we will discuss imposter syndrome in depth in Chapter 7, any time I feel like it was an accident, I remind myself how that one moment changed my life into something better. As with any accident, you are naturally unprepared because you didn't think it was going to happen.

Like Minded Females, also referred to as LMF or LMF Network, is the first business I founded. It's my entrepreneurial baby – a baby I didn't ask for, I sometimes couldn't afford, but I promised to look after nonetheless.

When is a side hustle no longer a side hustle?

Through 2019, I balanced (sometimes not very well) building LMF as a passion project and starting a new career journey. This was my third corporate role, one that I had gone after with new-found confidence. LMF was growing organically and even had a team of volunteers working behind the scenes. I felt both overwhelmed and excited. The future was strong. It was bright. It was clear.

As my love for LMF grew, my love for corporate environments lessened. No longer was I motivated by suits, ties and money. I wanted to create social justice, launch campaigns on diversity and help people build the career of their dreams.

I carried on developing the LMF Network as a 'side hustle' and passion project. Every time an idea came along, the team and I would find a way to turn that idea into reality. We created programmes around career development, financial literacy and confidence. We designed a global mentoring scheme that had 200+ people sign up across 18 countries. We curated our first film festival. Before we knew it, we had engaged with thousands across the world; launched a community base in Toronto and our first Canadian university society. By mid-October 2019, I had found a sense of self within my new community but was becoming less connected and driven by my corporate role.

And so, in November 2019, I decided to take the leap and work on the business and brand as my main activity.

In all honesty, I didn't know the first thing about starting or running a business. What was I meant to do and in what order? Despite spending £40,000 on a business degree at university, I wasn't taught how to complete a tax return. Much of what we are taught is theoretical – we must read before we try. My motto is *you must try and fail before you decide.*

My year of strategically winging it (SWI)

The year from 2019 to 2020 was what I have coined as my year of 'strategically winging it'.

In the traditional sense, 'winging it' is to do something without any practice. My shift in mindset was more about putting a process to this new-found power. The power was to say 'yes'. After being called out for being too noisy, the process was as follows:

- **Take a note of your five principles** – if you could be known or associated with only five things, what would they be?

- **Identify your number** – mine was 60. Meaning, if I thought I could do a minimum of 60 per cent of something, I would say yes and, well, 'wing' the rest.
- **Learn from each experience** – take stock and reflect on each yes moment. What did you do well? What could you improve?

Figures 1.1 and 1.2 give a breakdown of some of the most significant achievements that I strategically winged, which got me to here; writing a book, sharing my story and preparing you for entrepreneurship.

My biggest *oh wow* moment was being able to deliver two TED Talks in the space of six months; 2,500 people go on the TED stage each year and I went on it twice.

In 2021 I started the year launching the LMF Network's mentoring programme, which was highlighted in the press as the 'largest virtual mentoring programme to be launched by a charitable organization' with 600 participants across 14 countries. Alongside this success, we were able to obtain a £9,000 grant, for which we had been rejected three times, I was scouted by Monki to appear in an International Women's Day campaign, and shortlisted for the *Forbes* 30 Under 30 list in Europe.

FIGURE 1.1   Strategically winging it in 2019

2019					Delivered my second TEDxTalk: Failure Comes Before Resilience
	Delivered my first TEDxTalk: Please Come Online	Commissioned by PwC for my first diversity training workshop			
JANUARY	APRIL	AUGUST	OCTOBER	NOVEMBER	DECEMBER
Invited to BBC Radio 5 to discuss Brexit		LMF Network hosted first brunch in Malaysia	Commissioned by KING in Berlin for a diversity workshop on neurodiversity		

FIGURE 1.2 Strategically winging it in 2020

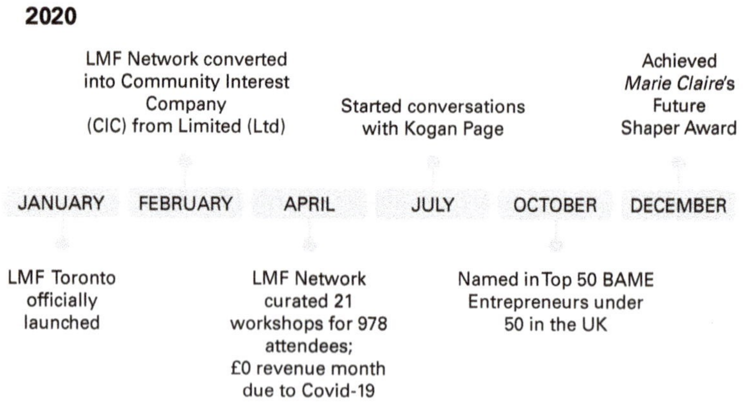

2020

LMF Network converted into Community Interest Company (CIC) from Limited (Ltd)		Started conversations with Kogan Page			Achieved *Marie Claire's* Future Shaper Award
JANUARY	FEBRUARY	APRIL	JULY	OCTOBER	DECEMBER
LMF Toronto officially launched		LMF Network curated 21 workshops for 978 attendees; £0 revenue month due to Covid-19		Named in Top 50 BAME Entrepreneurs under 50 in the UK	

I didn't come from wealth. I am of Pakistani heritage and the first in my family to attend university. I was raised in a fairly working–middle-class family and emigrated to the UK at age four. That world wasn't set up for me to succeed, but I took things into my own hands and created one that worked for me. **I took a chance on myself.**

What's the worst that can happen?

Nobody is waiting for you or cares enough to define your identity, ideas and beliefs. That's all on you! Preparing to be an entrepreneur starts with identifying who you are, your grey area and level of frustration. It then moves to shifting your mindset, taking a chance on yourself and setting yourself up for success.

Figure 1.3 shows how I expected entrepreneurs to ride out their waves, assuming that the process was simple and straightforward. However, in reality the journey is far more complex and exhilarating. You never know what the hurdle may be, but you will have jumped over enough to know you can jump over another.

FIGURE 1.3 The hurdles of becoming an entrepreneur

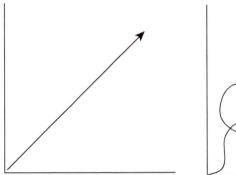

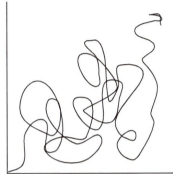

The expectation of entrepreneurship   The reality of entrepreneurship

Saying that, the next few chapters may be a bumpy ride. There will be times you will want to take a break for a breather. This is okay and encouraged. It's a marathon, not a sprint.

Stay with me and let's make magic together.

Are you ready?

EXERCISE

This chapter was an introduction to entrepreneurship, in which I hope I have shown you that if I can do this, so can you! Before we move on to Chapter 2, take a moment to note down how your life is today and then envision how it will be in 12 months' time. Make a chart and jot down the progress you would like to see. You're on a journey, so it's important to know where you are starting from and where you plan to go.

WORKBOOK

_____

_____

_____

_____

_____

_____

_____

_____

_____

_____

_____

_____

_____

_____

_____

_____

_____

_____

_____

_____

_____

_____

_____

_____

CHAPTER TWO

Entrepreneurship – nature or nurture?

As a toddler, I would drive my grandfather to worry, standing up in my pram, walking on the pavement edge and going on every funfair ride I could access, just so I could see higher places. I was too small to see the world from where I was, so I would try to climb and gain a new perspective. That was the creative fix to my problem – to jump onto ledges so I had a better view.

I used creative methods to find solutions and was determined to make them work. This determination has been carried through into adulthood and has fuelled my entrepreneurial journey.

Creativity is the key to starting a successful business. Here are three questions to get you thinking about entrepreneurship:

- Why are you interested in entrepreneurship?
- What is one problem you remember wanting to solve as a child?
- If you could solve that problem now, how would you do it?

I grew up on a council estate, with very little understanding of the world. My father hustled daily, and my mother raised four kids while running the family home. The TV was always on in my house, generally on the Disney Channel. Every show's family dynamic appeared to be very put together and poised, with big houses and beautifully maintained lawns. The characters I was trying to relate to would always have the best clothes and the newest toys. They were constantly going to the movies, attending baseball games, shopping at the mall or ordering takeout (which in my household was a real treat). The television shows never represented my reality, but they inspired me to do better. Here, the madness begins.

My mother met her best friend in the grounds of our primary school, while taking my brother and I to school. My brother and I befriended her children, and each week we would get together and create games to play. I would often let my imagination run wild to solve a challenge. We didn't have a garden slide, so we would take a mattress to the top of the stairs, sit on it, and slide down as if we were in a play gym.

This creative spirit in children resembles the entrepreneurial spirit in adults. And this same spirit shouldn't be lost in comparison, competition or fear of failure.

In my opinion, entrepreneurs are not born but made – often by unlocking their creative minds to form solutions in an ever-evolving landscape. It is a maddening lifestyle, but for many of us, it is the only choice. Without realizing it, I have been massaging my entrepreneurial muscles from a young age, never labelling it more than just child's play.

This chapter will focus on what style of entrepreneur you are, what creative exercises will help formulate your business idea and how to turn that idea into a tangible business model.

Are you unlocking your entrepreneurial style?

It took me a few months to appreciate my entrepreneurial style. This style, flair and pizazz were new and uncomfortable. I didn't know what kind of entrepreneur I was, I wasn't prepared for the logistics and, well, my business model was far from being complete. For many founders, the business model evolves as they grow. Establishing your entrepreneurial style is key to keeping your business innovative – otherwise, you can lose your passion, drive and style.

Initially, when I decided to create the LMF Network, I teamed up with a friend and envisioned a global not-for-profit model that focused on reducing inequalities faced by women and marginalized communities in tech, digital and entrepreneurship. Our key themes included positive change, social good and social mobility.

In 2019, I decided to leave the toxic corporate world and build this dream life. After 12 months of transitioning from just a thought, to a passion project, to a side hustle, to the dream life I had envisioned for myself, I thought I would be happy and fulfilled. Turns out, I was bored and frustrated by month three.

But why? I started to chase the money and base each decision on finances. The idea wasn't a pyramid scheme in the making, and it also wasn't a business that could sustain its growth. Within three months of becoming an 'entrepreneur', I had shifted my focus to money. In all the books I have read and podcasts I've listened to, I couldn't find anything that spoke about losing your passion so early on. I remember feeling lost and entertaining the thought of shutting down.

A stroke of luck arrived in the form of a UK-based business accelerator course for 'social impact' companies. They offered me a spot. It was the first time I had heard of such a thing. I walked in on day one as a limited company and left the same day as a community interest company (CIC). It took me eight hours of hard work and no technology to return to the core objectives of the business.

I re-identified my entrepreneurial style: a combination of a hustler and social entrepreneur. Once I was able to define my entrepreneurial style and the business model's direction, the other business areas became more precise, relevant and easier to navigate.

Styles of entrepreneurship

There are five styles of entrepreneurship we should consider:

1 innovative;
2 hustler;
3 social;
4 imitator;
5 intrapreneur.

An **innovative entrepreneur** is someone who is continually coming up with new ideas and inventions. They often aim to change the way people think or live. These people are motivated, passionate and obsessive. The thing that makes innovators stand out is the originality of their ideas.

A **hustler entrepreneur** is continuously working towards the bigger picture. They often start small and work hard to solve problems with their own resources rather than raising capital, and pool resources in creative ways to meet their needs. More often than not, what drives their ambitions is a lack of something.

A **social entrepreneur** is someone who wants to solve social problems with their products or services. Their goal is to drive positive change in the world rather than achieve big profits or wealth. These entrepreneurs tend to start not-for-profit organizations or charitable companies and dedicate themselves to social good.

An **imitator entrepreneur** uses existing business ideas and aims to improve them. Their purpose is to make sure products and services are better and more profitable. This entrepreneur is a combination of innovator and hustler. They are ultimately solving problems with a prototype that already exists. Imitators are self-confident, determined and learn from others' mistakes.

An **intrapreneur** fosters an entrepreneur's characteristics for a large-scale organization to create and lead improvements to increase profitability. This person has the security of a salary, the backing of an established brand and the freedom to innovate services or products. Gifford Pinchot coined the term intrapreneurship in 1973. In his 2017 blog, he shares four more ways to define an intrapreneur: 'employees who do for corporate innovation what an entrepreneur does for their startup; dreamers that do; drivers of change for good and self-appointed general managers of new ideas'. This entrepreneurship style is essential to highlight. It's a viable alternative to independent entrepreneurship, especially if you conclude that you aren't ready to build your own business after reading this book.

These five types are not rigid – there is no right or wrong route to entrepreneurship. However, it's important to allow yourself to think creatively while building your business.

When did you last have a business idea?

According to Tseng and Poppenk (2020), humans have 6,200 thoughts per day on average. Imagine out of all those thoughts, one of those ideas could be the difference between your current life and your future one. Which one will it be and why?

My mind tends to wander and daydream. I can take even the smallest thing out of context and conceptualize it into something else. During my life in the corporate sector, this skill wasn't considered favourable; as an entrepreneur, it's allowed me to stay alert and active.

The idea behind my consultancy business came to me when I realized that LMF Network was never going to make me rich (or somewhat financially stable). I found myself with two new businesses by March 2020 – a commercial, profitable model and a community-led social enterprise. It fed my alter egos – the social philanthropist making change and the wealthy socialite bringing in the cash.

A primary research poll I conducted on LinkedIn in 2019 found that 78 per cent of entrepreneurs don't start businesses because they don't know where to start but really, all you need is an idea. I encourage you to note down all ideas or potential concepts in your phone, on a notepad or on a sticky note and pop it on to the fridge!

Think about the following:

- What was your last idea?
- Under what circumstances did you form that idea?
- What did you do with that idea?

If we go back to our younger selves, we were good at scrambling things together to keep ourselves entertained, sometimes ditching the options that we were given to create new ones. My niece would rather play with a piece of paper or throw her food on the floor than play the piano that I bought her. The innocence of kids trying new things, such as pretending their stairs are a slide, is the type of imagination that can lead to innovation. We must retain this mindset as entrepreneurs. It can help us identify our grey area, a clear solution and reasoning why – all important first steps.

I distinctly remember shoving good business ideas under the rug up until a few years ago because I believed they didn't fit the 'mould'. These ideas included a home delivery box that would contain goodies to cheer you up when having a bad day, a data-led platform that supports partners buying gifts for their other halves, and a blog called *womanish* that covered the everyday life of being a (non-stereotypical) woman. I even bought the blog domain, before freaking myself out and shoving it under the rug.

There is no such thing as a 'mould' or a 'character' fit for building a business. Anyone can be an entrepreneur. Building a business is not about perfection, but about creating something around your hypothesis.

I don't have a business idea

Creating an idea is stepping out of the box, as Giovanni Corazza suggests in his 2014 TEDxRoma talk. He asks, 'why are you going out of the box to create an idea?' The box is safe, comfortable and nurturing. This move from the known to the unknown is what sets us apart from the nine-to-fivers. Think about all the things around us that were just an idea at the beginning. Who thought of mixing flour and water to create dough? Forming a 'like' function on social media to give us instant gratification? Taking a picture from the front camera and calling it a 'selfie?'

In the last few decades, scientists have been working on the theory that creativity is due to your brain's various networks connecting and working together as a team. The brain has three different networks:

1 Default network – the inactive mode.
2 Executive network – the decision and emotion centre.
3 Salience network – this determines what you notice and what you don't.

Dr Grant Brenner suggested in an article in *Psychology Today* magazine in 2018 that 'the three networks must operate as a team' in order to facilitate creativity. He explains that the 'default mode network generates ideas, the executive control network evaluates them, and the salience network helps identify which ideas get passed along to the executive control network'.

Creativity isn't something one is born with but a skill that can be strengthened by everyday experiences. Watching films, reading books and writing things down can be a way to train your creativity muscles. Start to draw out new habits you can practise from today: can you think of a new way to do a daily task? How about playing the 'why' game and asking why to everything until you can't any more?

A method to the entrepreneurial madness!

The method I recommend you use is made up of four simple steps:

1 Identify your problem.
2 Form an idea to solve that problem.

3 Present a quick, lean business plan.
4 Prove your solution to be either right, not relevant, or to be improved.

A trait all entrepreneurs have in common is that the majority started their journey by identifying their problem. It's important to find your grey area and then colour over it with your favourite shade.

What I have come to realize is that to stand out and survive as an entrepreneur, your idea must excite you and seep into your dreams. This idea may take over your life, but will be so strong that you will aim to give it a go at all cost. The *giving it a go* mentality is the underlying method to entrepreneurial madness.

How do you articulate your idea?

Making your idea a reality may be tough, but articulating it is even harder. Especially if you already have a 'kind of business idea' but aren't quite sure how to define it. The main drivers when articulating an idea are purpose and substance. Let me tell you from personal experience, as someone who has failed more than she has succeeded, nothing works if it doesn't have substance.

Before we begin, make sure you have the following ready:

- a piece of paper or some Post-it notes, and some pens;
- good connection to the internet and no distractions.

My advice is to give all of the following methods a try – you have nothing to lose.

Write down as many answers as you can think of to the following questions:

- What is the problem you are trying to solve?
- Whose problem is it?
- Why does it bother you?

Now, take this same energy into the two following exercises, which you can use to flesh out your idea.

Choose your method of madness

1. POSITIVE MIND MAPPING (FINDING THE BEST IDEA)

Mind mapping is a design method used by teams to generate ideas and free thinking within a controlled environment. There are some limitations, such as time. Mind mapping is a non-judgemental, out-of-the-box exercise that ensures that all solutions are covered from each angle.

SIX STEPS TO CREATE A VALUABLE MIND MAPPING SESSION

1 **Set a time limit** – the Pomodoro Technique is a proven technique used worldwide to increase productivity when finishing tasks (Cirillo, 2020). You set yourself a defined time limit with no distractions and take a break only after you've completed this block of work. The recommended time to set aside is 20 minutes.
2 **Bring the discussion to life** – pick material that will allow creative juices to flow. This can include the following: a whiteboard and coloured pens, sticky notes and paper, or your laptop's paint function. You want to leave feeling inspired and motivated.
3 **Quantity over quality** – put down on paper as many possible solutions as you can.
4 **Weird is wonderful** – the weirder the idea, the more unique it is. Unique selling propositions are a core element to making a wonderfully entrepreneurial idea come to life.
5 **Define your hypothesis** – a hypothesis is your explanation or proposal with limited evidence. It's the reason your initial idea exists, or what it is solving. For example, the reason this book exists is because my hypothesis was that 'there aren't enough accessible business stories out there'. I was tired of seeing the same people online telling me how they started their businesses (without sharing any real insight).

6 **Finish to filter** – once the timer has finished, stop. Work through each of the ideas and group them under similar 'umbrellas'. This will allow you to filter them into 'buckets' and eventually narrow them down from many to just a few.

By the end of the six steps you deserve a pat on the back! Your mind-mapping session has (hopefully!) been a wild ride, ending with an idea (or a few) which you can consider taking forward.

2. NEGATIVE MIND MAPPING (FINDING THE WORST IDEA)

This is mind mapping turned upside down because instead of the best idea, we are starting with the worst. Sometimes it's easier to know what doesn't work than what does.

SEVEN STEPS TO FINDING THE WORST POSSIBLE IDEA

1 **Define your problem statement** – find a solid 'problem' statement that you can unpack. For example, 'I feel alone and have no one to talk to about career progression'.
2 **Set a time limit** – as discussed above, taking into account the Pomodoro Technique, I would recommend setting aside 20 minutes.
3 **Control the narrative** – list all the possible solutions to your problem statement, with minimal detail, that you can think of within the given timeframe.
4 **Detail the bad ideas** – for each 'bad solution', write down the logic behind the solution. For example, building a community group that charges £100 per event.
5 **Consider the opposite** – for every bad idea, write down a positive or opposite quality. For example, having an accessible community group.

Don't worry about the time for the next two steps:

6 **Swap the solution** – swap each bad characteristic for a better solution.
7 **Mix and match** – think of this solution as your own personal mix and match, to find what complements a good idea.

By the end of this exercise, you should be able to generate ideas that could be potential business opportunities moving forward.

Let the idea or possible solution cook for a few hours. When you revisit it with new energy, test the water and see how it feels. Is the solution still tangible?

If working in a team, please remember to include everyone in the process as this will bring different perspectives to the table. Different personality styles may dominate the conversation and it's important to bring different ideas into the mix by asking questions or inviting the quieter colleagues to share. We cover leadership styles in Chapter 7.

Turning your idea into an action plan

Once you have found your set idea, it's time to dive further into the details and consider all the other elements. As an entrepreneur, the most important thing you can do is get your idea out of your head and into a tangible format to understand each element of your business. The simplest way to do this is by using the Business Model Canvas or the Lean Canvas model. Both of these models can be found online.

What is the Business Model Canvas?

The Business Model Canvas is an online business tool used to visualize the nine building blocks needed to start a business. It was created by Alexander Osterwalder, a Swiss business entrepreneur, and is a template to document your clientele, value propositions, finances and more. It lays out visually how an organization creates, delivers and captures value. The Business Model Canvas is widely used. However, we will be using the Lean Canvas model, which is a more efficient and trimmed-down version created by author Ash Maurya.

The Lean Canvas model

A fundamental factor of the lean approach is to eliminate waste. This waste includes, but is not limited to, time, process, inventory and fear. The Lean Canvas model uses the same nine blocks as the Business Model Canvas but is modified to deliver value and continuously refine the idea. The Lean startup model is validated learning through a continual build–measure–learn feedback loop, as explained in Figure 2.1.

WHAT ARE THE BLOCKS ON THE LEAN CANVAS?

Each Lean Canvas block is explained below, in the order that they should be filled out:

1 **Problem**

Each business solves a problem. Without a problem to solve, you don't have a product/service to offer. In this box, list three high-priority problems.

FIGURE 2.1   The Lean Canvas model

Problem	Solution	Unique value proposition	Unfair advantage	Customer segments
Top three problems	Top three features	Single, clear, compelling message that states why you are different and worth buying	Can't be easily copied or bought	Target customers
	Key metrics Key activities you measure		**Channels** Path to customers	

Cost structure	Revenue streams
Customer acquisition costs Distribution costs Hosting People, etc	Revenue model Life time value Revenue Gross margin

PRODUCT	MARKET

2 **Customer segments (CS)**
   The problem and customer segments are intrinsically connected – without a CS in mind, you don't have a problem. Your customer segment is simply your ideal or target customer, whom you believe this business solution will help. We will discuss this in greater detail in Chapter 3.

3 **Unique value proposition (UVP)**
   A unique value proposition is a promise of value to be delivered. It's the primary reason a potential customer should buy from you. A way to get your head around this is to think about why you and your business are different to the rest and why your CS should buy/invest time in you. We will cover brand value and perception in more detail in Chapter 5.

4 **Solution**
   Finding *the* solution is what's going to make you profitable! Finding *a* solution is what will keep you afloat! However, you're probably not going to get this right the first time. That is okay. The right solution will come over time, after innovating, failing and trying again!

5 **Channels**
   Channels are ways for you to reach your customers. Your main channels should be online. More can be found on this in Chapter 4.

6 **Revenue streams**
   Running a business only works if you can generate income long term and in a sustainable way. Revenue streams are the number of different ways in which your business can gain and maintain cash flow. More on this can be found in Chapters 9 and 10.

7 **Cost structure**
   Consider all costs, such as the website build, social media content, technical software and daily business expenditures.

8 **Key metrics**
   Key metrics monitor performance. These can include revenue per client/member, client retention and profit margins, to name but a few.

9 **Unfair advantage**

A great definition of unfair advantage is 'A real unfair advantage is something that cannot be easily copied or bought by your competitors' (Maurya, 2021). What do you have that no one else does? What makes you different and special?

The LMF Lean Canvas model

One of the reasons I wrote this book was because of my own pitfalls. In the early stages of my entrepreneurial journey, I had faith that I could do something, I just didn't know how to begin. I hadn't set out to start a business, so a planned approach wasn't a priority of mine.

Without clarity of my business model or a real purpose, I failed to attract any initial community members, and almost lost my passion. The business model took far longer than it should have, because I was too afraid to sit and write down what I actually wanted.

Writing this book has taken me on a journey with my business and myself. The entrepreneurial muscles have transformed into something tangible. It's weird how life works. With our whole model shifting online, income was lost and yet so much perspective was gained. We went from nothing to something in 18 months.

Figure 2.2 is a representation of our Lean Canvas model.

I will break down this full Lean Canvas model into individual snapshots and walk you through each of them.

The first snapshot looks at the problem, solution, existing alternatives and key metrics section, as shown in Figure 2.3. The key problem identified was that there are limited resources for networking on career conversations globally that are accessible and inclusive. The solution was to build this community with an incorporated mentoring programme and to obtain advice from

FIGURE 2.2 The Lean Canvas model applied to LMF Network

Problem	Solution	Unique value proposition	Unfair advantage	Customer segments
1. Networking around career conversations is expensive 2. People feel lonely and without community 3. Many have no access to mentors	1. Accessible inclusive resources 2. Mentoring programme 3. Supportive community channels	A real community network founded by real people who have lived experiences of the problem	Understanding of the problem through lived experience	18–35-year-olds Women Marginalized communities
Existing alternatives	**Key metrics**	**High-level concept**	**Channels**	**Early adopters**
1. Online membership clubs 2. Forums such as Reddit or Facebook groups 3. Localized mentoring	1. Follows 2. Engagement 3. Mentoring participants 4. Partner organizations 5. Shares of content	Diversity network with life skills programme, mentoring scheme and supportive community forums	LinkedIn, website, Slack, Instagram, in-person, online	16–28-year-olds, unsure about the future, their career goals and are looking for guidance from those experienced

Cost structure		Revenue streams
Online tools Gmail Zoom	Marketing and social channels	Time and effort of those involved
		Donations Funds Grants Partnerships

FIGURE 2.3   A snapshot of the Lean Canvas model

Problem	Solution
1. Networking around career conversations is expensive 2. People feel lonely and without community 3. Many have no access to mentors	1. Accessible inclusive resources 2. Mentoring programme 3. Supportive community channels
Existing alternatives	**Key metrics**
1. Online membership clubs 2. Forums such as Reddit or Facebook groups 3. Localized mentoring	1. Follows 2. Engagement 3. Mentoring participants 4. Partner organizations 5. Shares of content

FIGURE 2.4   A snapshot of the Lean Canvas model

Unique value proposition	Unfair advantage	Customer segments
A real community network founded by real people who have lived experiences of the problem	Understanding of the problem through lived experience	18–35 year olds Women Marginalized communities
High-level concept	**Channels**	**Early adopters**
Diversity network with life skills programme, mentoring scheme and supportive community forums	LinkedIn, website, Slack, Instagram, in-person, online	16–28-year-olds, unsure about the future, their career goals and are looking for guidance from those experienced

others. The existing alternatives included expensive membership clubs and localized mentoring forums, which didn't take into account the globalization of the current workforce.

The second snapshot covers the unique value proposition, unfair advantage, customer segments, high-level concept, channels and early adopters as shown in Figure 2.4.

My unfair advantage was that I lived through the problem. I understood the reasons this would be an issue or cause adverse consequences. The proposed customer was an 18–35-year-old who identified as a woman or came from a marginalized community. In reality, the early adopters were 16–28-year-olds who felt lost and were looking for guidance. The high-level concept was to become a diversity network with a mentoring programme, shared through LinkedIn, Instagram and the website. Soon, we realized it was better to focus on one or two channels.

Finally, the third snapshot, shown in Figure 2.5, includes the cost structure and revenue streams. The basic costs in the beginning were online tools, marketing material and the people involved. Proposed revenue streams were donations, grants and partnerships. In reality, all three revenue streams were difficult to obtain as I wasn't able to predict financial projections over a longer period of time and as a consequence of COVID-19, as these proposed revenue streams had additional barriers to access.

The Lean Canvas model helps get your initial thoughts down on paper to see if they make sense. Being an entrepreneur is about making sense of your idea and being able to articulate it, as much as it is growing the business.

FIGURE 2.5   A snapshot of the Lean Canvas model

Cost structure			Revenue streams
Online tools	Marketing and social channels	Time and effort of those involved	Donations Funds Grants Partnerships
Gmail			
Zoom			

Own your madness with a method

This book is best used in stages. Take time to reflect.

By the end of this chapter, you should have understood basic business models and concepts, and learnt how to mind map and build your own business model. You may be feeling exhausted or exhilarated. Whatever the emotion, congratulate yourself for coming this far. We are playing the long game here. Between the tortoise and the hare, slow and steady always wins the race.

CASE STUDY   David Savage

In 2015, David Savage founded and started producing one of the largest technology podcasts in Europe, titled *Tech Talks*. In his day job, David works for recruitment company Harvey Nash. He understood the recruitment market and wanted to reinvent it. He decided to create content that spoke to and energized his clients. Initially, there was reluctance from his employer to support the project, so David decided to do it himself. Fast-forward six years, and Harvey Nash has given *Tech Talks* its own website, platform, entity, budget and direction. David's motto is to 'ask for forgiveness, rather than permission'. You can find his business model canvas online on my personal website for reference, under the section 'book'.

What problem were you trying to solve with Tech Talks?

As a recruiter, you find yourself offering the same product as others. Getting in front of a customer is challenging. Initially, this was about getting in front of potential customers, and making them excited to spend time meeting me; perhaps even flipping the process and getting potential clients to ask to meet me. This was to get them excited about the technology industry, and process and convert them from curious to prospective customers.

How did you identify your audience and value?

The market (recruitment in technology) was already defined by my role at Harvey Nash. However, I felt from the events I attended that there was an audience looking for insight that wasn't getting the best information and value it could! That was the grey area – the sweet spot!

People want to talk to and receive validity from their peer community.

Why did you use a podcast format instead of another product or service offering?

It was a very low barrier of entry and was a medium I was capable of upskilling myself in relatively easily. It didn't cost much and was not as prominent in the UK market as today. The first podcast was recorded on my phone and edited through free software (Audacity). I made it very clear to customers that the recording wasn't the end product but talked them through the process and what I was trying to achieve, which they appreciated.

What challenges did you face?

A lack of track record or any real experience in podcasting, hosting or creating content. A lack of audience too, initially, especially as it was a new idea and one that was still being validated; it was created under a different brand to the Harvey Nash group and led by myself. Credibility in content is often afforded through consistency, which takes time.

What did you get wrong, if anything?

The length of the podcast was too long with no real focus. I couldn't edit on the spot, I wasn't consistent and I worried about what the show *should* be – a business podcast? It took time to let it find its own voice. As much as the brand and business have their own identity, which takes time to find, so does the service or product.

How did you change your company's mind from reluctant to supportive?

As a business, one of the major KPIs is profit, and the podcast took me away from my day job with no immediate return on investment (ROI). I work in a sales organization with a short sales cycle, with activity that has clear outcomes and this wasn't so clearly defined. I believed it would drive value, but I needed time to prove that. Eventually, I curated a couple of episodes, which I was able to share with them. I understood that this wasn't business critical and so worked on the podcast outside of work hours.

What are the benefits of being an intrapreneur?

Security of a salary, expertise to lean on in the organization around you (if you have relationships where you can tap into that knowledge), a brand or platform to build on. I found intrapreneurship worked for me, as it allowed me to be a business owner, build a brand and take risks, with the comfort of another brand as a security blanket. The podcast is now recognized as its own business unit with a budget, and its branding intact.

What tips would you give to someone starting a similar business or venture?

The first 10 attempts of anything you do aren't going to be very good. It doesn't matter. Keep going, remind yourself of the problem you are solving, the grey area you've found and why this matters! Always have open, transparent conversations taking your customers, clients or company on the journey with you and never feel that you are alone. Also, I performed the Lean Canvas activity and found it very helpful, both for refreshing the idea as to why I started and reminding me of the end goal – I would recommend doing a similar exercise every six months to track your progress and stay motivated.

What opportunities have been brought forward by this idea?

I am now widely recognized as an industry expert and a capable event/panel host/interviewer. That means I get placed in a room with all sorts of people who, five years ago, I wouldn't have dreamed I'd speak to as a peer. That's a wholly different dynamic and it has fundamentally changed the trajectory of my career. Intrapreneurship has allowed me to build a brand, business and name for myself with the security of my company, as well as take them on the journey.

Afterthoughts

David's reflection on the Lean Canvas method brings to light the importance of having a clear vision and plan, even if it's to look back at when times get tough. Intrapreneurship feels like a recent development in business, although it's been the basis of many entrepreneurial ventures. David's experience is a reminder that entrepreneurship doesn't need to be solo. You can keep the security of employment, and build something new.

WORKBOOK

_____
_____
_____
_____
_____
_____
_____
_____
_____
_____
_____
_____
_____
_____
_____
_____
_____
_____
_____
_____
_____
_____
_____
_____
_____

CHAPTER THREE

Does your customer understand who you are?

In the past, I have found it challenging to articulate my value, skills and strengths to other people. I have always tried to fit in by imitating others or adapting to my surroundings – often losing myself in the process.

Entrepreneurship has taught me that you are not only convincing someone to buy into your business but asking them to buy into you, your values and your story. Consumers want to know what makes your business unique. As an entrepreneur, your main unique selling point is you. It's what makes your company/business/brand different from your competitors.

This chapter will cover the value proposition concept by introducing exercises to identify your core customer, alongside covering the number of ways you can read, translate and execute the data that you have gathered.

Value yourself

What is your value proposition and to whom will this be of interest?

Your value proposition is a fundamental part of your business. It is the narrative that tells your customer why they should pick you over a competitor. Consider this: why does someone pick Samsung over Apple, Nike over Adidas, or Uber Eats over Deliveroo? The companies have very similar offerings, designs and databases. However, they appeal to different clientele.

Peep Laja, founder of CXL Marketing (2019) shares that 'a good value proposition can be read in under five seconds'.

What is a value proposition?

A value proposition is a concise statement highlighting how a product solves a problem or improves the customer's situation. It is a clear headline, attracts the right prospects, increases the quality of leads and provides clarity regarding messaging. Lastly, it communicates why your customer should care about your business, product or service. According to Alexandra Twin for Investopedia (2020) 'a customer value proposition is a promise of potential value that a business delivers to its customers and in essence, is the reason why a customer would choose to engage with the business'. A good value proposition should cover:

- What is your business?
- Why does it exist?
- What problem does your business solve?

WHAT IS A BAD VALUE PROPOSITION?

The following are not parts of a value proposition:

1 **An incentive:** The word 'incentive' is defined as a 'positive motivational influence' designed to prompt a visitor to act right away. Incentives are not value propositions.

2 **A catchphrase:** Often referred to as a slogan or tagline, Shukairy (2019) on *Invesp* suggests that 'a catchphrase is a small group of words that are combined in a special way to identify a product or company'. These are often catchy and memorable.

3 **A positioning statement:** A positioning statement is an expression of how a given product, service or brand fills a particular consumer need in a way that its competitors don't. A positioning statement is a subset of a value proposition, but it's not the same thing.

Building a good value proposition can take tweaking and time, but it's key to your success.

Evolve to meet your customer's needs

If I were to ask you to close your eyes and imagine your ideal customer, who would they be? Now, open them and write down who you saw.

Customers are essential to all businesses, regardless of whether you are a profit-led or not-for-profit business. If you stop engaging with your customers or fail to make them see how you meet their needs, your business will fail.

I used to go to Blockbuster every week with my parents to rent a DVD. It was a kid's paradise, with aisle after aisle of all the latest movies and video games. Reed Hastings tells Marketplace (2020) about a relevant anecdote from his new book *No Rules Rules* (Hastings and Meyer, 2020), which outlines the story of Netflix. He shares that in the early 1990s, as a newcomer to the DVD rental space, 'Netflix asked Blockbuster to buy the business for £50 million'. This offer was declined by Blockbuster and Hastings goes on to say that that night he went to bed and 'I had this image of all sixty thousand Blockbuster employees erupting in laughter at the ridiculousness of our proposal'. Years later, Blockbuster failed to keep up with consumers' digital demand, and Netflix became the go-to streaming platform and a household name. In 2021, Gail Kellner on *Go Banking Rates* reported that Netflix's estimated net worth is $30 billion.

This story illustrates:

1 **Adjust to the pace of innovation.** Technology is revolutionizing how we do things, but it's up to you and your business to adjust. A great example of this is TikTok, the short-video-generating content platform. At the start of 2020, TikTok was a reasonably new app in the UK, but quickly became the social platform to use. The short video content changed the social media narrative, and soon Instagram was releasing its own version. If Instagram had not adapted its model, it could have potentially lost customers and lessened its value.

2 **Use data to drive your decisions.** The great thing about starting a business today is that there is so much tech out there to help you understand your customers' needs. Data can be collected by conducting surveys and Instagram polls, and using Google Trends.

Your ideal customer cares about your product, solution and business. They are waiting for you to enter their world and take them on a journey. At the same time, it is vitally important that you care about your customer and ensure their needs are met by truly understanding what they are. This means conducting research, caring for their needs and being aware of trends.

Let's find your customer

Each decision you make should have your customer in mind.

Consider the following questions when planning your next move:

- How will this benefit my customer?
- How will this engage a new prospect?
- Is my solution going to solve their problem?

How to create a customer persona

A customer persona is a high-level description of your ideal customer. It includes assumed characteristics, with distinguishing pain and gain points, say, young, urban women aged 20–30. Pain points are the problems your customer is facing and gain points are how your business will solve those problems. By defining your customer persona, you can create better products to solve their problems, curate marketing to support your brand's growth and consider special offers to build loyalty. While you may not have a defined customer persona when you start thinking about your business, you should start with at least an idea of who you want your customer to be.

Follow the exercise below in order to create customer personas. You may consider having more than one target customer persona, which is often the case with businesses. If so, I encourage you to have three (maximum) in mind. Any more may be a detriment to your business model.

The three steps to creating a customer persona are:

1 **Identify** the problem your business is solving.
2 **Understand** who needs this solution.
3 **Create** their persona on a one-page template. I have included a mock-up of this in Figure 3.1.

What information should you include?

- **Personal information** – name, age, socio-economic and educational background.
- **Professional information** – industry, role, employment status, location.
- **Pains** – what problems do they have?
- **Gains** – what solution will your product or service provide? Which goal of theirs will you help them reach?
- **Reading and social media habits** – which digital platforms do they use? What kind of content do they consume?
- **Motivations** – What is this person motivated by? What drives their passion?

FIGURE 3.1   Customer persona

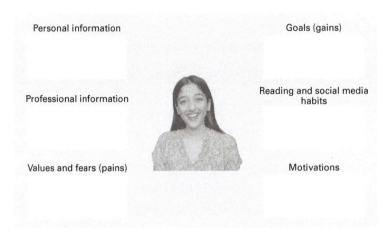

At the start of my business, I didn't consider who the customer was. It took me three attempts to get this right, and even then, it wasn't perfect. Initially, I thought my customer looked like me. However, it turns out my ideal customer is any person living through similar experiences and pain points rather than someone who identifies as a twenty-something woman. These biases and assumptions meant that I had to go back to the drawing board when things didn't go as planned.

You can consider your presented customer profile as a hypothesis that you're aiming to prove or disprove through market research and validation.

How do you validate your customer?

Market validation is the process of determining if your product, service or brand is of interest to your customers and target market. There are a few techniques that can be used to assess market interest, which we will discuss.

Validating your product before going into mass production is cost-, resource- and time-effective.

How do you create and validate your market research?

Before becoming an entrepreneur, market research scared me. It seemed like this massive unachievable task that would cost more money than it would earn back in return. However, like most others, I overcomplicated the concept. If you are a small or new business, you can't expect thousands of responses right off the bat. Market research and validation are about being relevant, clear and gaining a representative sample that you can work from. There are a few different data points you can use when conducting market research.

Quantitative data answers the 'who', 'what', 'where', 'how' and 'when'. It is numbers-based, whereby linear numbers represent people's feelings or thoughts, for example, 'On a scale of 1–5, how likely are you to follow our brand?' **Qualitative data** includes feelings, opinions and written text. This is often harder to measure, though important, as it answers the 'why'. This can be, for example, 'Which social platform do you prefer and why?'

The different forms of data available include primary and secondary data. **Primary data** is the data you get when you conduct the research yourself. **Secondary data** already exists and can be found via reports, public forums or other online sources. One method is to use secondary data to prove or disprove the bulk of your assumptions, either by building case studies or using it as a reference point. Primary data can be used to collate additional or new insights, which can be specific to your brand or business. For example, in 2021, the LMF Network conducted a research study around diversity and inclusion within the workplace. Rather than generate a full report based solely on primary data, secondary data was used to build the premise and story, while the preliminary data was presented to counter or agree with the original findings. Using both data sets is beneficial to your research and enables it to be foolproof.

WHAT DIFFERENT PRIMARY DATA METHODS ARE THERE?

1 surveys;
2 polls;
3 interviews;
4 focus groups.

Surveys are online or in-person question-based forms that are sent to customers to fill out. There is no limit to the number of questions you can ask in a survey. However, I recommend keeping it clear and concise to encourage more people to fill it out. In-person surveys give you the option to talk to the person face-to-face, which can sometimes work to your advantage. In 2019, I helped a new London-based startup gather market research by encouraging them to take to the streets. Within one hour, they had interviewed 100 participants, which helped direct their initial website design.

Given that 4.66 billion of us have access to the internet (Statista, 2021), **digital surveys** are often more accessible. Using free tools online such as Google Forms, Qualtrics or Typeform, you can create a short survey and shoot it to your network through online channels.

Polls are tools used to understand people's needs through a voting system. Polls are now available on most social media platforms and are often free to use. You can create a poll to understand your customers' needs through your social account and theirs. Polls on Twitter and LinkedIn can be live for up to seven days, whereas an Instagram poll exists only for 24 hours in the stories function. UN Women is an example of an account that often uses polls to understand its followers' concerns around complex topics such as violence, safety and gender inequality. These polls form the basis for events, workshops and programmes.

Interviews are qualitative forms of data collection that include sitting down and asking another person questions. This is the most time-consuming method but generates the most significant amount of data. For better results, interview questions should be prepared in advance. Interviews can be conducted offline or online through free tools such as Google Hangouts, Zoom or Facetime. Record the interview so you can listen to it later and transcribe the conversation.

Focus groups are an extension of the interview process that involve more than one person. Similar to interviews, these can be conducted online and offline in groups of up to 20 people. I recommend using the free digital tool Slido to ask questions, and have the answers form their own word cloud. The great thing about word clouds is that they automatically change the font of the 'word' associated depending on how many people have anonymously shared it. I used this technique to identify the current working and diversity situations during my workshops for King and Soldo, which greatly benefited my work. Focus groups can be as effective using digital tools as conversations in person. Consider using WhatsApp, or alternatively try WeChat or Telegram. One thing to note is that in focus groups some respondents may have a stronger voice than others, so it's up to the interviewer to manage and navigate a fair conversation.

Beauty Pie Founder Marcia Kilgore describes the idea of Beauty Pie as 'something that came to her one afternoon in a Milan train station, as she was making her way back from a beauty manufacturing region in Italy known as "Lipstick Valley"'. She left wondering why the real cost of beauty products wasn't reaching customers directly, when they could be getting a great deal for luxury beauty if companies were to remove mark-ups. Marcia took her 'idea to the doorsteps of beauty editors, to test it straightway, who initially reacted with disbelief. There was certainly education that needed to take place'. Beauty Pie values customer feedback through social channels and polls, to ensure that strategies and products continue to live up to its value proposition, which is to democratize access to luxury beauty. Marcia's relationship with the customers has also enabled Beauty Pie to create beautiful and photogenic packaging while keeping in mind the aim to be as ecologically conscious as possible. Marcia adds that she 'doesn't believe in launching companies just to launch them, but to develop an idea that improves the daily life of a customer'. Beauty Pie and Marcia's story is a good example of how your idea can be validated by asking potential customers and the impact such feedback can have in evolving the business product and service.

What do I do once the data is collected?

If your data is handwritten, type it out in Microsoft Word or Google Docs. If it's in a Google Form, move it into an Excel spreadsheet, and if it's a poll on social media, take a picture and transfer it into written text. Next, it's time to understand what has been captured. When displaying the data, play around with different graphics, pivot tables and visual tools such as word clouds. If you have a large sample set and are comfortable exploring new tools, I'd recommend using the accessible version of Tableau or Qualtrics.

Once you have collated your data, you can then use the information gathered to prove or disprove your hypothesis. Your hypothesis in this chapter is to prove or disprove your customer persona, but on a broader scope it can be the business model, problem, solution or marketing campaigns.

Data can drive your decisions. There are no right or wrong answers. This often throws people off, as it can be pretty uncomfortable not knowing what you will find out. On the other hand, proving or disproving what will work for your business before investing the time, effort and funds will only be beneficial for your brand or business.

Let data drive your decisions

If, as Clive Humby said, 'data is the new oil' (Bridle, 2018), let's use this rich currency to enhance your product, service or brand.

Consider the next few chapters as a part of the validation process.

1 **Create a landing page** – Using the data you have collected, create a landing page with your business information.

2 **Produce samples** – If your product is physical, consider sending it to potential customers. This can be done through market stalls, advocacy through word of mouth, or gifted social media campaigns. The Coconut Collaborative, a dairy-free dessert company, offered new products and flavours to neighbouring businesses in a weekly giveaway that ran on social media. The initial campaign focused on brand recognition, but they also found this to be a great way to test their product on a small budget with their prospective customers.

3 **Use test ads** – Digital advertising, which we will cover in depth in the following chapters, is a great way to test your idea on a limited budget. Creating campaigns using advertising platforms such as Google, Taboola or Facebook is a quick way to confirm if your business, brand and value proposition work the way you intended. For example, A/B testing allows you to create two similar campaigns with one unique differentiator: the campaign title, value proposition or customer demographic. The results can support your argument for moving forward or trying again.

These fundamental business stepping stones are important before the business becomes tangible. There is often a whole new level of excitement felt when bringing your idea to life and giving it its own identity.

Making your brand a reality

What is the name of your business?

Your business name needs to combine your purpose, brand concept and offering into one nifty word or sentence. A bad business name can impact your growth. Finding your business name requires brainstorming and patience. My advice is to identify a few words, concepts or sentences that define your solution and start merging them to see what sticks. Look up synonyms in the thesaurus and see if they sound better. Don't be afraid to think big. The name 'Like Minded Females' was came about when my partner joked about the brand and value proposition. It was at that moment the lightbulb turned on above my head and I had a real 'ta-dah' moment. My next step was to jump on the internet and google it to see if it already existed – it didn't. And so, I bought the domain name, created a logo and set up an email address.

In hindsight, I soon learnt that although one thing means something to you, it may not to anybody else.

My business's name also had its own biases. It was exclusive to 'Females'. Though this was the model at the start, all genders, intersectionalities and identities started getting involved. The name felt wrong. This drove me to change the name to the LMF Network as an inclusive abbreviation.

Unfortunately, in December 2020 our brand domain name wasn't auto-renewed and while in the process of ordering a new business bank card, the domain went back on sale and was picked up by a bot. Long story short, the *likemindedfemales* domain is now on sale for £10,000. Ironically, it was the push we needed to rebrand the whole community network and the business.

As an entrepreneur, the simplest of tasks can often feel the hardest because they seem so simple – like keeping on top of your subscriptions. I can only suggest that in order not to go through what I did, make a note of all your subscriptions, their renewal dates and regulations in a private document.

Fortunately, our value proposition was secure and our brand strong, so we didn't lose as many customers as we thought.

How do you create the visual side of the brand?

Because of my excitement and lack of experience, I didn't think much about the brand, colours or consistency at the start.

I created the logo using Canva's free logo tool, picked the colours that spoke to me and designed all content based on what I liked.

According to research by Kurt and Osueke (2014), colours come with their own associations and are 'fundamental to sight, identification, interpretation, perceptions and senses'. For example, red is considered to be fiery and strong. Blue is more transparent and passive. It's important to also note what colours mean in different cultures. For example, black is often worn in the UK at funerals as a sign of mourning. In China white is seen as a sad colour.

When I started LMF, our primary colour was light pink. According to Bakhshi and Gilbert (2015), images with a dominant colour of red, purple or pink have a higher chance of being shared by other users. However, we soon had customer feedback to suggest that the lighter shade of pink wasn't inclusive or bold, which contradicted our message. For this reason, we as a network conducted an Instagram poll to understand which colours our users would prefer.

Unanimously, the results were that a darker, more coral shade of pink was preferred, bringing the notion of strength, boldness and character. Funnily enough, the coral was Pantone's colour of the year in 2019 and cultivates a sense of energy, community and becoming comfortable with yourself (The Chalkboard, 2019).

Take time to focus on the visual element of your brand, including colours and messaging. Do your research, ask the audience and sleep on your decisions before driving them into the core business brand. If they don't fit your messaging, you will have to redouble your efforts and try again.

How to create a website

The core purpose of your website at this stage is to have a basic design that outlines three things: the problem you are solving, how you are solving it and where people can purchase the solution. Consider your website as a work in progress.

Initially, I'd recommend using templates on Wix, WordPress or Squarespace to design your website. Don't overthink the content. Focus on getting your core message down on the page, with clear links in case someone wants to make a purchase or contact you for more information. Websites cost money, so you should be ready to invest some budget.

The great thing about technology is that you don't need to be a coder or an engineer to create a website design. All the sites mentioned above have a 'no-code' element, which means that you don't need code to create the site, but can instead use a ready-made template, which can then be edited.

Setting yourself up for success also means setting yourself apart from the competition, and much of that will be directed by your customers, communication and campaigns. Since becoming an entrepreneur, I have found that many people have amazing ideas that aren't as great when put to paper because they are unable to articulate them or they don't meet the customer's expectations.

CASE STUDY   Son Chu

In this chapter, we meet Son Chu, co-founder of Rens Original, the world's first coffee sneaker. The sneaker is waterproof and made from recycled coffee and plastic. Son Chu is originally from Vietnam and resides in Finland. He met his co-founder Jesse Tran through his job, having finished his studies in Finland. One year after their initial meeting, they decided to launch their footwear business Rens, with a vision to make sustainable footwear fashionable. Son is recognized by *Forbes* magazine as one of the 30 entrepreneurs under 30, 2020.

Where did the inspiration for Rens come from?

The footwear industry tends to be bound by what existed before. As a basketball fan, sneakerhead and young person serious about sustainability, I was surprised that there wasn't a product that already existed combining all three elements. I wanted to wear something fashionable and high tech, while also taking care of the environment.

Why did you land on making sneakers out of coffee? Strange concept, for many.

Yes, not many people know that coffee beans can be recycled to create fibres. We tried different yarns, such as recycled plastic, bamboo and charcoal. However, coffee seemed to fit best with the design. The coffee yarn has been used in products such as beanies, hoodies and sweatshirts, but never sneakers. The ironic thing is that coffee is the most consumed drink in Finland and one of the largest Vietnamese exports, so it felt like a natural fit of the two worlds.

How did you produce the first sneaker and was it love at first sight?

Honestly, my co-founder and I spent one year researching fabrics, materials, products and manufacturing partners before we got to the design. We then created an MVP (most viable product) and took it to the streets of Finland. It was very helpful to receive first-hand feedback from our proposed target audience and hear what they liked or didn't. Much of the first prototype's feedback was that it was too bulky – this was the case as we wanted it to be waterproof – but it wasn't stylish. As we wanted it to be stylish, waterproof and sustainable, we went back to the drawing board.

You mentioned your target audience – who were they then and who are they now?

Great question. Our initial audience was us – young professionals aged 24–35 years who wanted to be fashionable, trendy but environmentally friendly. Our ideal customer would have money to spend on shoes and be interested in fashion. In reality, our actual customer falls into a larger age bracket starting from 18 years of age and has disposable income, which isn't for impulse but considered before spending. Much of our target market was assumed and then confirmed through digital advertising, campaigns and going out onto Finland's streets.

Tell us more about how you conducted market research and confirmed your customer

Market research is fundamental to each and every business. We (my co-founder and I) made a prototype and asked everyone we could for feedback. Based on this feedback, we created a new version and conducted the same exercise. Considering our target market was mainly using Instagram as a social tool, we decided to launch an Instagram page and campaign, targeting our demographic through advertisements. This helped to elevate our brand and drive awareness while giving us results of which designs, patterns and products worked. As I mentioned before, we took to the streets to ask people, randomly walking up to them with our shoe and asking questions. It's imperative to conduct research for your own sanity and to avoid wasting money, in the grander scheme of things.

Were you and your co-founder always aligned on the destination for your business?

We are young entrepreneurs and have gone from being colleagues to CEOs. No one really tells you about that experience. I am still learning my managerial style, as well as nurturing my co-founder relationships. My co-founder and I are different people with the same vision. It's important to have the same vision and align. We sometimes have to fight for what we want, but on the condition that if you get your way, you must prove it works. This means, if I was given the green light on a design or marketing campaign, I would still have to prove its worth within let's say three months before either progressing or handing it over to the other idea. Working with another person is great as you can bounce ideas off each other.

What is the one piece of key learning you'd like to share?

Make an MVP and test this through active campaigns, from going out and asking people, all the way to digital media campaigns, before you invest all your life savings. Too often we hear business and founder stories of entrepreneurs who sunk their savings because they didn't clarify their value, customer or reason for being.

Afterthoughts

It was reassuring to hear that Son Chu and his co-founder took to the streets to gain customer feedback before investing their savings into their business, for no other reason than to make sure it made sense. Your value proposition and customer narrative can be reformed once you are in a position to understand them and can speak directly to their needs. As entrepreneurs, we must acknowledge that we don't know everything but we are willing to learn. Son's honesty is refreshing. It reminds us to not stagnate. To grow your business, you must also grow as a founder, business owner and brand. The only way to progress on the path that will eventually lead to success is to ask your customers, colleagues and consumers for their thoughts – these are the same people who will be paying for the end product. In the next chapter, we will discuss how to launch your brand on social media, gain traction, find business opportunities online and grow your community! I'm so excited to be on this journey with you.

WORKBOOK

_____

_____

_____

_____

_____

_____

_____

_____

_____

_____

_____

_____

_____

_____

_____

_____

_____

_____

_____

_____

_____

_____

_____

CHAPTER FOUR

Social media for your business

According to Statista (2021), 142 minutes a day is the average amount of time a person spent on social media in 2020, a 30 per cent increase since 2015. In 142 minutes, an average person can cover two 5k runs, bake four loaves of banana bread, or travel to Amsterdam from London Heathrow.

Given these numbers, I can make a bold statement: *without social media, your business cannot prosper.* If 50 per cent of the global population is on social media (Roser *et al*, 2021), can you afford not to be?

Yet, it's not as easy as it seems. In 2019 I decided to launch and manage the Instagram channel for LMF Network. I went in excited, I walked out exhausted. I was terrible at it.

I was so bad that the LMF handle even got blocked – potentially because the account had no clear purpose. I thought, 'how hard can social media be?' It was very hard, because I didn't know what I was doing.

Eventually, in January 2020, we relaunched the account, with a new brand and team (more on this in Chapter 6).

Here are three social media lessons I learnt the hard way:

1 Have a clear brand narrative, otherwise people may not believe your business is real.
2 Understand your customers' problem and communicate how your business helps to solve it.
3 Identify a clear metric of success, which goes beyond the number of followers – not all followers convert into customers.

Community engagement on these platforms can attract a loyal group of customers that care about you beyond the account. Customer behaviour has shifted – we are online, consuming information in shorter chunks and making decisions impulsively through digital content.

This chapter is about using social media as a tool to meet customers and building a strong brand presence to achieve customer loyalty. Consider social media the bridge between your brand and your customer.

Should I believe the social media hype?

According to SWEOR (2021), businesses have roughly 2.6 seconds to make an impression using visual social media content. The hype is real.

What is the purpose of being online?

A business social media account without a purpose is a waste of time and resources. By defining the goals you hope to achieve with social media, you can weave it into your marketing strategy and link it to a key performance indicator (KPI) as a success metric.

The main purposes of being online are: to conduct market research, identify trends, build brand awareness, drive traffic, generate leads, drive sales and build community.

To conduct market research and identify trends

Conducting market research is the first step to building your brand online. Social media gives you the ability to track current and emerging trends. One way to do this is by monitoring current hashtags or topics that are trending across platforms. Before launching the LMF Network's new Instagram, I took a few weeks to follow relevant hashtags to understand what other brands were doing. These hashtags included #community, #business, #motivation, #diversity and #mentoring. I purposely left them broad to appreciate the full spectrum of content that was being shared.

We used Instagram polls to understand if our new brand colour palette was favoured by the community and LinkedIn polls to identify how long our Lives should be. From these polls, we decided to commit to a darker shade of pink and 30-minute LinkedIn Lives.

You can also identify trends by following trending topics on social media channels, or using tools like Google Trends or other free trends-based data sites such as Sprout Social, Hootsuite or Buffer.

To build brand awareness

Brand awareness is the extent to which customers are able to recognize or recall your brand. Examples of brands that have nearly universal brand awareness include Coca Cola, Apple and Starbucks.

Once customers interact with your tweets or Instagram posts a few times, they'll start to get a sense of what to expect when they visit your social media page – whether that's design or tone of voice or something else entirely. I experimented with red, pink and black within social media posts, workshop training decks and even the branding of the book. Using the same colour palette across accounts, I was able to distinguish myself as a brand.

To drive traffic and generate leads

Posting on social media will drive people to your website, sign-up sheet or any other online destination you want. Traffic creates potential customers. One way to ensure traffic is by linking your website or business page in your social media posts.

How do you drive traffic?

- create content relevant to your audience;
- promote this content with a clear call to action;
- use relevant hashtags or search terms that you believe your target market will be looking for.

I created a reel on Instagram titled 'How to overcome imposter syndrome'. I posted it online because I had seen more conversations happening on social media and through community groups than in real life. It seemed to be impacting one of my target demographics – women in the workplace.

This reel was viewed by 30,000+ people and converted into three commissioned workshops within a three-month period.

This form of primary research also allowed me to share my expertise with others. Eventually, a number of people who viewed my post messaged to ask if they could share it within their businesses, and if I was able to run workplace training on the topic. This led to an Instagram Live with Bocan luxury wear and two workshops with the BMW head office.

To convert leads into sales

Once you have encouraged your audience to view your product offering or website, it is now time to convert that lead into a purchase. This type of conversion is part of the marketing funnel. Sophia Gibson, a marketing and operations specialist who works with startups and entrepreneurs explains: 'The marketing funnel is made up of five stages – awareness, interest, desire, action, and loyalty. When promoting your product or service, you want as much awareness as possible. This is because the stages start to reduce in size as we work our way down the funnel. The greater the awareness, the more chance of an action being carried out.'

How do you convert leads?

- develop a relationship with your consumer;
- provide an incentive, a promotion or highlight your offer;
- direct them to buy it.

Natalie Furness, a British business owner and marketing expert, states that leads can be captured using customer relationship management (CRM) tools such as HubSpot or MailChimp. She shares that 'CRM systems sit at the heart of all customer-centric businesses and contain personal information on each customer'.

For easy sharing and accessibility, Natalie recommends using a 'cloud-based CRM system. To ensure that every customer record is kept updated. Support staff use CRMs to address customer queries. Marketing teams use CRMs to personalize communications to customers. Sales teams use CRMs to identify sales opportunities and account teams use them to identify and chase up late payments.'

For the LMF Network, we use CRM tools through platforms such as Wix, Flo newsletter and Eventbrite to track customers and their engagement.

To build a community

By building a community, you are able to create a forum to innovate, share ideas and gain feedback. An engaged community can also help you change your perspective and build brand loyalty. Brand loyalty can lead to word-of-mouth recommendations, referrals and repeat business. The concept of community-building is still relatively new and is discussed in depth in the next chapter.

How to build a community:

- identify which platform best serves your specific audience;
- invite members into the community and promote this as a group with clear guidelines;
- start conversations, follow up on comments and engage with content shared.

Jasmine Douglas, the founder of Babes on Waves, uses Instagram as her main tool to build a community. She tells me that 'an audience is made up of people who you talk to, whereas a community is a group of people who engage with your content on their own and talk to each other. Instagram is the tool I use as that's where my audience is. I share content and generate new ideas, before inviting these people into discussion forums, events or into the members' club.'

Social media is easier to manage when it's your primary focus. However, as an entrepreneur, you have limited time. You may find yourself overwhelmed with social media and unsure of where or how to start. To make things easier, I encourage the following steps:

1 **Identify your primary and secondary social tools** based on where you believe your most loyal customers are. For example, I would use LinkedIn and Instagram for my personal brand. LinkedIn because it is the largest business platform, and Instagram because it is relevant to my company's target audience of 18–35-year-olds.

2 **Outline two to three goals** for social media use and keep them SMART: specific, measurable, ambitious, realistic and time manageable. For example, this could be to increase the number of followers by 25 per cent every quarter.

3 **Give yourself eight weeks** to build and maintain a consistent social media presence before checking the results. Social media analytics are richer if you have given yourself ample time to build the brand.

As with anything in business, you will get social media wrong and that's okay. It's better to fail fast and learn fast.

How do I pick my primary social tool?

There are hundreds of social media apps and tools available. Depending on which country or city you're in, you may even have localized versions of each major site. I have identified and categorized the five types of networks that currently exist and how they can influence your business.

The social five

Social networks are popular networking tools such as Facebook, Twitter and LinkedIn. Social networks are often referred to as 'relationship' networks and are used to connect with people and brands online. They help make one-on-one connections and build community.

Business entrepreneur Rebecca Page transformed her passion for sewing from scratch into a business via Facebook. Her story highlights how quickly a community and business can grow when you take a moment to listen to people's needs and harness the power of social media to share your message directly with them. Rebecca used Facebook to 'launch her business and understand what other people do when wanting to sew products from scratch and started a group to share insights'. Initially the group invitations went to people she knew who then invited others from their network. She goes on to explain that 'After an organic growth period, the business generated new leads by offering free trial patterns, encouraged new followers to share their designs and introduced them to brand ambassadors who shared their creations'. A passion project to full-time business, Rebecca tells me that by 2021 'this community soon grew to 700,000+ members who became loyal business customers'.

Social media platforms focus predominantly on images and video content. These include YouTube, TikTok, Snapchat and Instagram. These networks are used to find and share live content, photographic media and videos.

Lara Sheldrake leads the online community Found & Flourish (F&F). This community was created on Instagram while Lara was on maternity leave and apprehensive about going back into the workplace. Found & Flourish provides community, connection and resources to entrepreneurial women. 'Originally, F&F was a community on Instagram to connect aspiring entrepreneurs with inspiring women founders,' explains Lara. Within two years, Lara converted the community into a membership subscription model. The success of F&F unfolded as it 'used Instagram to build brand awareness, grew audiences through the power of storytelling as well as generating leads through social events offline and online'. F&F also shared motivational images and videos on trending topics like work–life balance, freelancing and motherhood during the Covid-19 pandemic.

Discussion forums are those where you can find, discuss and understand trending news and questions. Examples include Reddit, Mumsnet, Hacker News and Quora.

Discussion forums have immense power in driving trends and can inform market research. At the start of 2021, a group of contributors on Reddit's platform drove up the share price of GameStop, a US high-street retailer that sells games and electronics. In two weeks, the stock boomed from $4 to $200 (Finnis, 2021) – all because of shared efforts on Reddit.

Customer review networks aggregate customer reviews and can highlight customer experiences. These include Yelp, Tripadvisor and Google Review.

Margot Vitale, the co-founder of Curate Beauty, shares that 'being an online platform, we rely a great deal on the trust of our customers'. During the Covid-19 pandemic, Curate Beauty was forced to shut down its pop-up shops in London and move online. In-person foot traffic disappeared, but Margot explains that positive reviews helped keep things moving: 'Google Reviews offer a peek into other customers' experiences with us, lending to new customers' trust in our business proposition and practices.'

Blogging and publishing networks are used to publish, discover and comment on content, and include WordPress, Tumblr, Substack and Medium.

Mo Seetubtim, founder of The Happiness Planner, initially started her business as a blog to inspire people to stay motivated. As it grew in popularity, she converted it into a newsletter, among a host of other products including productivity journals. 'In this way, I was able to capture data and generate leads,' explains Mo. 'I brainstormed ideas for a business model on the back of my content and customer base, and today have built a business with 500,000+ followers, creating custom journals for companies like Netflix, Deloitte and Bobbi Brown.'

She explains that 'blogging tools are a great way to enter the world of words without any commitment, as these are free. Once you let yourself write and share, you never know the opportunities it can lead to because you never know who's reading.'

What is the future of social tools?

In my opinion, digital marketing platforms are evolving and revolutionizing the way we approach brand awareness, social media communities and marketing. For example, during the Covid-19 pandemic we saw an exponential increase in video content and audio-based apps. The two winners (in my opinion) were TikTok and Clubhouse.

TikTok allows you to share video content up to 15 seconds in length to the global market. According to MediaKix (nd), this platform is mostly used by 16–24-year-olds, with the average user spending 32 minutes on the app. TikTok boomed during the Covid-19 pandemic, growing to over 800 million users monthly (Reitere, 2021). Brands that have been able to use this platform effectively to grow their user base include Gymshark and UEFA. Brands can use TikTok to create and feed adverts, and generate hashtag challenges, which generate social content through relevant trends.

Clubhouse grew from 1,500 users to 1 million within 12 months according to *Influencer Marketing Hub* (2021). This platform is audio only and brings together conversations from all over the world.

Estelle Keeber, founder of Immortal Monkey, shares that she started to use the 'platform with intention in February 2021'. She tells me that in order to make the most of the app as a business owner, spend some time 'researching into the different rooms and thought leaders who are on the platform. Know why you are using the platform: to learn, to educate or to listen. Set a time limit so that you aren't consumed by the platform, and go on it during different times because users are active all over the world.' As a working mother, Estelle has found benefit using the social app to create connections with experts such as the producer of *Despicable Me*, John Cohen. For new entrepreneurs, if you are wanting to see a return on investment, Estelle says to 'interact and engage continuously, sharing value and knowledge and building relationships'.

I must admit that while writing this book I tried my best to stay off the app but found myself borrowing an iPhone in March 2021 to enjoy the interactions. In my opinion, the fact that initially it was only available to iPhone users was a great marketing strategy as it built the fear of missing out (FOMO). However, on the other hand this meant that the app itself wasn't inclusive.

Similar to Estelle, I limited my time on the app, allocating only 15 minutes twice daily. I would spend the first couple of minutes scouting rooms to see which topics were of interest and where the speakers were limited, so I could try my chance on the stage. Once on the stage and sharing information, I would follow the other speakers and invite the audience to follow me. In order to convert these app-based connections into potential customers, I would find them on LinkedIn and send a friendly request reminding them that we met on Clubhouse. Through these interactions, I have been able to line up virtual coffees with CEOs from the United States and Asia, find potential brand partners and increase my visibility as an entrepreneur.

It's my opinion that digital social platforms are essential in establishing and evolving your business. Business ideas can be generated and proven through the interactive tools at your fingertips – and these tools are only becoming more precise.

Making social media work for your business and your brand

The core purpose of social media is to elevate marketing. Marketing is any activity that encourages consumers to buy into your product. In this section we will cover your brand identity, the four marketing Ps (old and new) and how data can drive your decisions.

Who is your customer and where are they?

When I first started the LMF Network, I assumed I knew my demographic before doing any market research. That's probably why we didn't start strong. Figure 4.1 lays out my assumptions about the target demographic versus their reality.

FIGURE 4.1   Assumptions versus reality

SOCIAL MEDIA CONTENT PLAN

	ASSUMPTION	REALITY
IDENTITY	Young women	18–35-year-olds, majority women (not limited to)
LOCATION	Living in London	Global, majority in big cities
PAIN POINT	Feel constrained by the barriers to progression in the workplace	Interested in upskilling their confidence, finding community and building capability. Not focused on immediate promotion but long-term progression
SOCIAL	LinkedIn	LinkedIn and Instagram

The exercise of identifying and validating the target market helped build and improve our social marketing strategy, align purpose and launch the network.

What is the marketing mix?

The marketing mix (4Ps) is a classic marketing theory that was created by E Jerome McCarthy (1971) and Philip Kotler. It defines the core elements required to market your business and brand: product, price, place and promotion. The marketing mix should allow you to meet your customer at their required place, at the right time, with the right price and solving the right problem. However, the marketing mix was created in a time before digital marketing and online forums. It's important to approach the marketing mix with an open mind.

The **product** in its simplest form is an item (tangible or intangible) to satisfy the needs of your clientele. It's recommended to do extensive research on your product to ensure that the end product is what's required.

The **price** is what the customer pays to enjoy the product or service. Pricing is important and depends on your business. If you are a social entrepreneur, your pricing might be free or affordable, ensuring everyone can join and a more inclusive community can be created.

The **place** refers to where the product or service will be distributed, from in-store to online channels such as Etsy, Amazon and Depop. Places transform greatly with the internet. The Covid-19 pandemic has changed the way food and drinks are distributed, with many brands who didn't offer delivery going online to accommodate for the lockdown, including McDonald's, KFC and Nando's, for example.

The **promotion** is the method through which customers find out about your product or service. Traditionally, this might have been through in-store advertising, and TV and radio advertisements.

Today, we are seeing promotion through community groups, social media, paid advertising, blogs, newsletters, influencer marketing and podcasts.

The following Ps are extensions of the mix, added by Dave Chaffey and PR Smith (2017), that consider the digital age.

The **people** are directly or indirectly involved in making the product or service – your team. They ensure the product is seen and purchased, and can include production, marketing, development, distribution and delivery.

The 'people' element expands into the **processes**. Processes are the various systems that a product goes through before it reaches the end consumer. This can include direct or indirect activities, such as feedback requests, back-office administration

FIGURE 4.2   LMF marketing mix

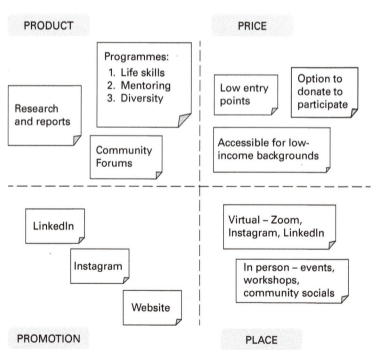

and service support. As a budding entrepreneur, the process is most likely yourself and any spare hands you can find to support you and your brand. Processes should be streamlined and documented to provide a reference point for new staff that join, or if you need to remind yourself of the best way to go about things. This also ensures you are able to iterate what didn't work into areas that do.

The **physical evidence** refers to everything your customers see when they interact with your brand. This includes the environment in which you provide the service, the layout or design, packaging and branding. This element can also refer to your workforce, how they dress and how they act.

The last P is **partnerships**. This includes the strategic brand partnerships between two businesses. For small businesses, this is a crucial factor in growth when resources are limited.

In Figure 4.2 you can see the marketing mix for the LMF Network.

The content road map

The most organized method for building social media content is to create a content road map or calendar, which will help organize your social media and business activity. You can start with pen and paper or an Excel spreadsheet. Your plan can then be uploaded to content tools such as Buffer, Hootsuite or Later.

In order to achieve the greatest impact, I would recommend investing a few hours every other week to plan, build and schedule the content for the upcoming week. I spend three hours every Sunday building the content for the LMF Network and my personal brand.

I spend time on the following five areas:

- **Setting the call to action** – what do you want someone to think, feel or do?

FIGURE 4.3 Social media content plan

	MONDAY	TUESDAY	WEDNESDAY	THURSDAY	FRIDAY	SATURDAY
THEME	Educate	Community	Enable	Community	Empower	Rest
FORMAT	Text graphic	Photo	Text graphic	Photo	Text graphic	Photo
TRENDS	#mondaymotivation	#tuesdaythrowback	#wednesdaywisdom	#thursdaythoughts	#fridayfeeling	#saturdayselfcare
LINKEDIN	LMF research	Past social event	Invite to workshop	Celebrate community success	Motivational quote	Article or interesting read
INSTAGRAM	'How to' slide deck with tips	Past social event	Invite to workshop	Celebrate community success	Motivational quote	Nature, park or something peaceful

- **Confirming the aesthetic strategy** – how will the content look and feel on your feed?
- **Finding trends** – what trends are boosting social media content and are relevant for your brand?
- **Organizing the content** – collate all the content in one file or folder to make it easier to upload.
- **Creating the captions** – personalize each caption to the audience and intent.

Figure 4.3 is an example of the LMF Network's content calendar, which is used among our many chapters to ensure we are consistent and customer-focused.

The content is uploaded onto these tools and set for automatic publication. Once posted, I spend 15 minutes daily engaging with comments, likes and queries.

I used to have moments where I'd find social media overwhelming and would confuse myself over what to post, given the sheer volume of content that already exists. Having a clear plan helps to de-cloud your mind and gives you focus.

Data analytics

Each major social media platform has its own free, in-house data analytics platform. After eight weeks, you should have shared enough content in order to gain valuable insights. The most important items you are looking for include content **engagement**, such as the number of **likes or comments**, brand growth through the increase in **followers**, and page **connections** and actual sales, through **conversions or items bought**. Platforms such as Instagram will also be able to share basic information on the types of users interacting with your content, including gender, estimated age and location. Similarly, LinkedIn will share their titles. These will add value when evaluating your social presence, understanding if your goals have been met and addressing future growth plans.

At LMF Network, we realized that our LinkedIn following consists of senior stakeholders who normally hold budgets and can make decisions. On Instagram, our following is largely young professionals. For our 2021 mentoring programme, we recruited mentors from LinkedIn and mentees from Instagram. This move helped us to launch the largest mentoring programme in the UK, with over 600 participants across 14 countries, as featured in TechRound (Dolden, 2021).

Today, we are online, consuming information in shorter chunks and making decisions impulsively. As new and small business owners, we must have clear messaging, customer-centric content and a clear value proposition. Building a social media presence takes time, dedication and data. It is a full-time role and you have to be in a position to invest a few hours each day. Don't be afraid to test, trial and challenge social media norms to grow your business, brand and boss status!

CASE STUDY   Chanelle Mauricette

Our social media entrepreneur is Chanelle Mauricette. Chanelle is a social media brand specialist, business psychologist and founder of influencer agency Novus Via Management. At the start of Covid-19, Chanelle focused on delivering motivational business content through her platform and within 12 months grew her platform from 3,000 followers to nearly half a million. This growth enabled her to quit her day job and run her own business.

What was your purpose for being online?

Initially, I didn't think much about social media as a tool to generate business conversations or brand presence, as I was invested in growing myself in the corporate world. However, once the Covid-19 pandemic hit, I saw more people leaning on social media for community and advice. With a background as a business psychologist, I wanted to help people understand what was happening in the world, how we could use the time to realign our current lifestyle with one we want and, most importantly, to place confidence in the community that all was going to be okay.

How did your purpose shift?

Once I started posting motivational caption-led content, I saw my following slowly increase as did my engagement. Having understood the basic concept of sales, I took some time to understand which trends were growing and what the concerns were for ordinary people through the pandemic. I hypothesized that my core demographic was women who required online support, a sense of community and ways to empower their daily lives.

What strategy did you use to grow your Instagram to over half a million followers?

I laid out a simple content plan and stuck to it for several weeks to see if it worked. After about eight weeks, I used the free analytics available on Instagram to see which content delivered the highest engagement and which didn't work. I realized that posts where I was able to focus on business-based content in fashionable clothing received the highest engagement. From this, I shifted my strategy to creating content with high-resolution imagery of myself in fashionable outfits, while keeping the captions focused on topics of interest such as business, empowerment, branding, community and mindfulness.

How did you go from full-time employee to full-time entrepreneur?

The growth of my brand was natural, as was the growth of the business. Through sharing content, I was being approached to lead training around personal branding, contacted by companies to come on board as a paid influencer and asked by numerous people how I entered the world of influencer marketing. From these conversations, I discovered that the market for influencer marketing was growing; however, agencies weren't working with diverse candidates nor micro-influencers as much as they could. This was the niche and business opportunity that I saw. I attempted to build what I thought would work as a social influencer agency in the background, contacted other micro-influencers to see if they'd be interested in coming on as our talent and agreed on working practices with my business partner, who I'd come to know through social media and online communities. This naturally grew through trial and error, which is the beauty of entrepreneurship.

How do you generate new business through social media?

The power of social media is such that once you have clear messaging and relevant content, it's not difficult to approach brands via their messaging tools or email addresses. I would estimate that 90 per cent of my business comes from Instagram and 10 per cent through LinkedIn, which is at the back of clearly identifying my customer market, their location and using that platform to build activity that you can share with them. Consider it your live portfolio.

What is one thing you want people to know about social media?

The algorithm is always changing. So don't compare your content to someone else's based on just the following. Conversion is more important than the number of people following you. Engage with your followers and build a community before you attempt to convert them into paying customers.

What happens when you get something wrong online?

Nothing. There is a constant fear of getting things wrong online, but the truth is that you must get something wrong to see what's right. There are plenty of examples where I have misread the room, audience or following, and shared content that hasn't delivered my measures of success. The great thing about social platforms is that they have free insights, so use your data to drive all decisions and reflect on what works, what doesn't and what will.

Afterthoughts

By using social media correctly, Chanelle has been able to work with large fashion brands such as Simply Be and I Saw It First as well as technology companies such as Lanistar. As leaders we must sometimes train our brains to think in line with business logic rather than emotions (read more in Chapter 7). If you don't speak to your customers, how do you know you're really delivering the product or meeting their needs?

EXERCISE

Before you move on to the next chapter, which is on community and networking, I would like you to identify your two main social platforms and build a content calendar that suits the needs of your customer. Don't worry about getting it wrong. This is part of the process. Iterate and evolve your social media presence as you evolve yourself as an entrepreneur.

WORKBOOK

_____

_____

_____

_____

_____

_____

_____

_____

_____

_____

_____

_____

_____

_____

_____

_____

_____

_____

_____

_____

_____

_____

_____

CHAPTER FIVE

Converting your network into your net worth

Without customers and a community, businesses and brands won't survive. The new way of entrepreneurship is to nurture relationships the same way you nurture ideas and skills. This is a running theme among many of the entrepreneurs I speak to. If it wasn't for our communities, our businesses wouldn't have been able to sustain any growth.

However, many entrepreneurs explained that their biggest hurdle is building their community and converting the people around them into consumers. These are the people who will actually use, share and champion your business, whether it's a professional community, which will connect you to future partnerships, mentors and hires, or your first customers who love your product so much that they share it with their friends. This community will keep you informed about their evolving needs, helping you iterate your product or service.

The right community can also grow your business. It's my belief that in 2021, someone is more likely to become a customer only after reviewing the experience associated with the business, perhaps by looking at online review platforms or comments on a brand's social profile, or asking their friends.

This chapter illustrates the importance of the three Cs – customer, community and conversation – and explores how to approach them along with social media. This will take your business to the next level.

Using the internet to find your community

Starting conversations on MSN Messenger

In 1999, when my parents bought a family computer, I was only allowed to use offline games like Solitaire and Paint. My siblings and I weren't allowed on the internet and were limited to an hour of daily activity.

It was only when I entered secondary school that I was able to enjoy the early experience of being online and connecting with friends. In 2004, I started attending a local girls' school. Every day, my group of friends would run home after school only to jump online and continue to talk to each other via MSN. Getting to know your friends online was far easier and cheaper than texting. Some of you reading this book won't know, but 'back then' in the UK, you were charged per text. Phones were only used to drop-call someone, hoping they could call you back – the real conversations were happening online. Friends would often add you to groups with other people, conversing on a similar topic such as GCSE exams or music. These conversations would slowly evolve into community forums, planned sessions of discussions, and convert into offline meetups in parks or libraries.

I also used MSN to keep in touch while I was away. As a family, we often used to spend our holidays abroad. During this time, it was MSN that allowed me to stay in touch with friends and my network, providing me with my first experience of maintaining a community regardless of location.

MSN Messenger was my first foray into relationship-building across the world. This is a key skill to use and develop as an entrepreneur.

How to find your community

Over 60 per cent of the global population has internet access (DataReportal, 2021). There has never been a better time to find your people, your circle and your community of customers online.

Each business's community is different and crafted to fit its needs.

LMF Network started as a closed group before opening up to the world. At first, we envisioned a brunch club to bring women together. We had a number of successes after double the failures; learning that our community existed outside of LinkedIn, for example, and were interested in building their capabilities, not just having conversations. Eventually, the network itself as a brunch club felt redundant because we had so much more to offer! The offering slowly shifted from conversations around a table to real educational workshops to build capability and training to foster inclusive cultures. Through this shift, I realized that the reason we were founded didn't quite align with the business reasons or goals. For example, we wanted to do more and commercialize the offering, so that all income could be reinvested into the community forums to generate more engaging activities. As we progressed into becoming a diversity network, which incorporated the community fundamentals with a business foundation, we found our niche and our power. Our purpose grew from being one thing to being something that could support people in different ways, all the way from educational content to accessible community events and discussion forums. Once our purpose was established and communicated, we thrived!

Who's part of your community?

As you get older, wiser (hopefully!) and grow into your role as an entrepreneur, it's important to assess your current circle versus the circle you want. Your immediate community is an extension of your network; it's the circle you hold dear or the group of people you actively choose to associate with. If you are surrounded by toxic people, your opportunities will be damaging. If you are around people who are on similar paths, your opportunities will grow, new opportunities will arise and you will flourish.

When I first floated the idea of the LMF Network by my friends and associates, many laughed or misunderstood its purpose. Did this bother me? Of course. Imagine your closest circle telling you the idea isn't good or worth considering. This is the reality for far too many of us.

As the seed grew into an idea, my need to surround myself with people who understood my mission and could support me became greater. I made the decision to surround myself with those who were more successful and knowledgeable than me. As a newbie to the world of business, I wanted to learn. Luckily, I relied on technology when starting conversations, creating connections and forming communities. This included simple things like following the right hashtags, connecting with inspiring entrepreneurs or networking within the community. It seems that I've come full circle from those moments on MSN Messenger, sharing my daily events as a young teenager, to an adult who is using the likes of LinkedIn and Instagram to build connections.

You may have heard the saying 'community over competition'. This proved to be true in 2020. With the global Covid-19 pandemic, online communities came together to support one another. I was invited to calls to support decision-making processes for businesses that weren't mine, contributed as an external interviewer as others grew their teams and was introduced to prospective clients after I suffered pandemic-related losses. Your network really is worth its weight in gold!

Is your network really your net worth?

According to motivational speaker Jim Rohn, 'you're the average of the five people you spend the most time with' (Groth, 2012).
Ask yourself:

- Who are the five people closest to you?
- Which opportunities are you seeking?
- Will these five people support you in achieving your goals?

Consider this alongside your current network. As I shifted to 'self-employment', I realized I didn't know where to start. Luckily, I had been able to build a network that I could reach out to. I asked all of the questions about starting a new company, from finding new business to filing taxes. From these conversations, I realized that one of the mistakes I made early on was not identifying clear success metrics. My community rallied around me, and set up meetings to guide me through the fundamentals of how to run a business. In the space of a few weeks, a friend led me through an exercise on how to have difficult business conversations, another reached out via Twitter to ask if I'd like to use her office space. Shortly after, another friend took me for a celebratory brunch and taught me how to fill expense sheets. Within four months, I gained new business friends, an understanding of basic business operations and understood how my community could help me stay afloat. Preparing to become an entrepreneur requires understanding your own knowledge gaps and asking people to support you in bridging them. There is no shame in asking questions. If you don't ask, you won't know.

My life changed once my network did. If you are the sum of the five people you surround yourself with, then I am extremely lucky to be in the same circle as my network. One of the biggest achievements encouraged by my network is this book. It was an opportunity that came through a connection in the form of an introduction on social media. Business friends, associates and community members are your allies. They do the work to support you, open doors for you and uplift you in times of need.

Three steps to going from nervous to networker

Networking isn't an easy task for everyone. I definitely have the gift of the gab, but that doesn't mean I am naturally gifted with the skill of networking. Here are three things I learnt from my journey:

1 Shift your mindset from negative to positive. In practice, this means going from 'what may happen' to 'what have I got to lose?'
2 Don't try to be everything for everyone at once. Conscious baby steps are the best way to build strong foundations before you try to run. Set yourself small, attainable goals, such as asking one person for an introduction each month, or reaching out to someone who inspires you for a coffee (in person or virtually).
3 Define your goal before you go into the conversation. Having a clear reason or agenda point makes it easier to send the request, follow up with an ask and convert it into a conversation.

Networking leads to opportunities

Networking can reveal business opportunities that don't exist on public forums. Research shows that 70 per cent of all opportunities are not published publicly and up to 80 per cent of those opportunities are filled through personal and professional connections (Freeland Fisher, 2020).

Networking does not need to be *just* transactional. Change the narrative and network to give instead of to gain. I approach networking as the 'art of listening, learning and leaning into someone's problems with solutions'. You receive three immediate benefits when you network:

1 The ability to create strong connections that can lead to things like partnerships and mentors.
2 The ability to openly communicate with others, trade ideas, and share goals and failures.

3 The opportunity to support the growth of your business and your connections' businesses through aligned goals.

During my first 'real' professional job, I remember being so afraid of networking that I found myself eating lunch alone. I always felt nervous about saying the wrong thing. It was difficult to start conversations with those I worked with, because I was afraid of not being smart enough. I felt like an 'imposter'.

On reflection, my lack of confidence spoke mountains about my self-esteem and identity. I realized that my anxiety came from being unsure of myself, my value and what truly made me special.

All it really took was shifting my mindset. With each situation, I tried to turn networking into one of my core strengths – a talent that I didn't believe I possessed. I've taken the stress out of networking, and instead focus on starting a conversation and listening. Even on weekends, you will find me sliding into someone's DMs (direct messages) and starting a conversation. I am making conversation with at least five new people daily through Twitter, LinkedIn or Instagram.

At the start of 2020 and my full-time entrepreneurial journey, I commented on a LinkedIn post from a person based in Amsterdam. I agreed with the topic they'd raised and shared my experience, with a clear email address in case someone wanted to get in touch with me. That one post was seen by the head of PR for a startup who then commissioned me for a training session for four other startups.

If I hadn't taken the risk, I might've missed out on the reward.

Personal branding and networking work hand in hand

Let your values do the talking

Before networking, it's important to assess your personal and professional values. These will also align with your business goals.

Daphna Oyserman defines values as 'internalized cognitive structures that guide choices by evoking a sense of basic principles of right and wrong, a sense of priorities, and a willingness to make meaning and see patterns' (Oyserman, 2015). Your values should be your guiding principles.

In order to understand your values, consider the following statements:

· What is your end goal, or the change that you would like to see in the world due to your business?
· What makes you feel happy?
· What makes you feel fulfilled?

Now, take a moment to dive deeper. Is there a connection between your answers?

For example:

1 My end goal is to make sure everyone can start their own business.
2 I am happy when I am having conversations with new people.
3 I feel fulfilled when I am able to share my learnings with my network.

Through this exercise, I understood that my common denominators and core values were accessibility, honesty and education. These are the three core morals my business, brand and even this book are built upon.

Understanding your core values is a healthy exercise to filter opportunities. We spoke about the values for your business in Chapter 2 and this same model can be replicated for yourself and your personal brand. If the proposal doesn't align with at least 60 per cent of your values, pass it on to your network. This way, you are focused, driven and conscious of your brand.

Defining values is also a key component of building your personal strategy. These values can help you plan your next move, lead your business into success and define measurables that are impactful. This is a long-term strategy. Building a business is a marathon, not a sprint.

Defining your value-adds

Many business owners shy away from sharing their stories online. The reasons range from not knowing how, to not thinking it's important. However, customers buy into stories. On social media, in order to leverage your network and convert them into an engaged community, you must start the conversation. One way of doing this is by telling your story and using it to identify your values.

In business, the term 'unique selling point' is often used to refer to things or tangible products that are different and a key differentiator for a service or product.

I'd like you to consider yourself as that business, service or product. Your 'unique selling point' might be your creative vision, your ability to empathize, your patient nature or your authentic voice. My unique selling point is I am able to bring a holistic view of community, companies and future capabilities, having understood what a lack of community can do for confidence, how companies are not inclusive and which capabilities are required for the future.

I grew my community by sharing my own negative experiences and learning process online. I have been commissioned by over 200 companies because I am able to use social tools to present my thoughts and arguments in a way that is beneficial for both businesses and diversity.

Introducing yourself, your brand and your business

We've covered the basic concepts of community, networking and values. The real challenge is condensing these into an impactful introduction that you use when you meet someone new.

At the start of my business journey, I used to cram everything I could into a 30-second pitch and hope the other person was following. I used to think the more I could cover, the better I sounded. However, that isn't true. It's about quality rather than quantity. To introduce yourself, you need to know what you want to be known for.

FIGURE 5.1   How to create your introduction in three easy steps

Consider the three core principles you want to be known for, your recent successes and accolades, and the goal you want to achieve from your new connection. That's your pitch. I've illustrated the process in Figure 5.1.

PRACTICE MAKES PERFECT
The first time you introduce yourself may be daunting and difficult. You may slip up and leave wondering if you said too much or not enough. Don't worry. This is normal. Practise in front of the mirror, record yourself on video or join random online webinars and start the exercise via the chat function. It will only get easier.

The internet is a wonderful network of things and people

Entering any situation without a clear definition of success is a big business no-no.

You're a business person, and you must think like one in all aspects of your work. If we take a page from the Lean Canvas model (Chapter 2), we start by considering our customer, our value proposition and our bigger picture. The next step is to ensure your brand and boss status.

Technology is in the palm of our hands and therefore should be considered a great tool to search for, interact with and make new connections. Since building a business online, one of the most important skills I have learnt is how to network. In 2020 alone, I upskilled over 2,000 people on how to use Linkedin effectively as a networking tool. Generally, the task here is to shift your mindset and use the internet as a way to generate new opportunities.

Having shared my experience and expertise with so many people, I have been able to gather the most common questions around networking, using technology and putting yourself out there. I have included some of them here.

What are the traditional networking steps?

1 Introduce yourself;
2 make conversation;
3 find a common topic/thread;
4 connect (either with business cards or on LinkedIn/through social media channels);
5 follow up;
6 grab a coffee (virtual or in person) and discuss how you can support one another.

Why should I network?

- **Brand awareness and exposure.** Though brand awareness and exposure can be difficult to measure, brands plan to increase their brand awareness in order to gain more customers.
- **Opportunities.** You want to make sure you're top of mind when someone in your network is asked for a referral or recommendation.
- **Access to resources.** Networks bring benefits including education and new ways of thinking. They can open doors to tools, resources and frameworks that you may not be familiar with.
- **Contacts.** Networking encourages meeting new people. A new network is a larger pool of contacts who know you, your name and your business. This can be beneficial in times of sale-generating leads or collaborating with others.

How do I politely decline a connection request?

I have to decline your offer as I am unsure how this will benefit us both.

No thank you. I keep my online connections limited.

Unfortunately, I don't think we would be able to support one another so I will have to say no.

There is no need to feel guilty about this.

What if I get rejected?

This happens and it's okay. In February 2020, I was seated in the cafe of the Mayor's office waiting for my next meeting. There was a lady sitting opposite me and we struck up a conversation. We spoke about education and changing lives by leading accessible programmes. I thought we were having a good conversation with similar views, so before she left I asked for her LinkedIn details. Looking me straight in the eye, she kindly declined, saying that there was nothing she could do for me. That was possibly the first time someone said no to connecting online. It was a humbling experience, a reminder that sometimes it's okay if things don't go the way you planned.

I'm an introvert, how do I network?

When I was interviewing Chanelle Mauricette (Chapter 4), she mentioned that she considers herself an introvert, meaning she is more likely to be reserved, take stock and be cautious when approaching certain scenarios. She viewed 'networking' as a 'character that you can switch on and off'. She recommended networking on your own terms, not someone else's. If you are introverted, manage your time and conversational points before heading into any networking situation; lead the agenda and don't be afraid to reflect before answering.

I've never had to network, so what's the need?

Networking should be embedded into your everyday practice. We are constantly talking to people, and networking is merely the next step; moving that conversation into one that is constructive and able to support and achieve your goal.

I'm a university student. Is networking for me?

Networking is fundamental for university students. While at university, I attended an open day for one of the UK's largest consultancies. During the afternoon tea break, I struck up a conversation with local staff about technology and data. They gave me some key pieces of information, which led me to secure an interview for a role I had my eye on.

How do I introduce my idea, especially if it's in the early stages?

The beauty of business is that no ideas are 100 per cent complete. If they were, new models and upgrades wouldn't exist. Start the conversation with your concept and the problem it's trying to solve. As long as you can clearly define the problem statement, then you've introduced it well.

Do I need a business card?

There is no right or wrong answer to this question. In some countries, business cards are preferred. In others, it's old-school and a waste of paper. I'd recommend printing 100 and always having a handful in your pocket, just in case.

Top tip: LinkedIn has a QR code function that can be accessed via the search bar, which you can use to scan someone's LinkedIn code or they yours, as an alternative to the business card.

What are some common barriers or challenges faced?

Common barriers we create for ourselves include thinking that the other person won't respond, fear of rejection and feeling like an imposter. These feelings are natural, but don't let your internalized barriers stop you from meeting other people.

What are some conversation breakers to avoid?

Avoid the following if you want a constructive conversation and connection:

- Going on about your business, brand or self.
- Making a definitive statement without explaining your position (eg 'this has to be done').
- Listening while multitasking (eg checking your phone messages as you listen).
- Rolling your eyes or displaying other uninterested body language (such as crossing arms).

How can businesses convert conversations into potential leads and customers?

- Adding all emails to a CRM system.
- Organizing catch-up calls with your top ten connections monthly to see what they need support with.
- Providing free or taster products before charging full prices.

Building your net worth using templates

Online networking has become particularly easy, because there is now the opportunity to use templates to send introductions, and the time to formulate replies. Here are some that I have used before, which have landed me introductions, conversations and even customers.

Starting the conversation

ONLINE

Hi _____. My name is _____ and I work in _____. I am here today because I am interested in learning more about _____ or

connecting with people in the _____ industry who I can help with
_____. Great to be in this online forum with you all!

Sending a connection request to:

SOMEBODY YOU HAVE MET AT AN EVENT

Hi _____, it was so great meeting you at the _____ (event/
workshop/webinar name). The conversation about _____ really got
me thinking more about _____! I'd love to stay in touch and hear
about what you're up to.

A THOUGHT LEADER OR INDUSTRY EXPERT

Hi _____, I've been following your content and I'm so impressed
with all you've accomplished. I recently read/listened to an
interview/watched a video of you, I'd love to discover more about
your work and support you!

A RECRUITER OR JOB-RELATED CONNECTION

Hi _____, I see that you work for _____ (name of recruiting/job
agency). I wanted to reach out because I'm currently exploring new
opportunities. I've been working professionally in _____ (name
of industry) for _____ (number of years), and I'm so ready for my
next big challenge! If you have time, I'd love to talk about whether
my background would make me a fit for any openings you have.
Thanks!

ASKING FOR A COFFEE/CHAT

Hi _____. Thanks for the connection! I have seen your work and
find it inspiring! I am interested in learning more about _____ and
so wanted to ask if you are able to schedule a 15-minute virtual/in
person meeting next week? Does _____ (day) at _____ (time) work
for you? If so, please let me know your email address and I can
share a calendar invite.

CASE STUDY   Kanwal Ahmed

I met Kanwal over Twitter in 2020. I had heard of her and her community, Soul Sisters, through my mother, who got involved via Facebook and found comfort in the online forum. When her Twitter handle popped up on my screen via a retweet, I decided to slide into her DMs. What was the worst that could happen?

> Hi, hope you are well. My name is Sonya Barlow and I am the founder of the LMF Network (@LMFnetwork) in the UK, similar to Soul Sisters in PK. I have heard a lot about your community through my mother, and loved the fact that you are making a difference in PK! I too am raising awareness of societal issues through LMF and now would like to give back to the PK community in some way. Wondering what I can do to help, would you be free for a chat? Thank you, Sonya

She replied to my message within a few days, and we planned a call. Since then, we have supported each other and have found comfort in sharing community wins and fails.

Kanwal Ahmed is a Pakistani entrepreneur who founded her community online in 2013. She used Facebook to find similarities between women facing societal issues in Pakistan, created a private group to start discussions, enabled a community using Meetup-style events, and eventually transformed her private social forum into a business. Her expansion model includes charging global brands to share products, hosting informative events and presenting her talk show on YouTube. The Soul Sisters community network grew from 0 to 300,000+ contributors in five years and has become the inspiration for many community membership sites today.

How did you create Soul Sisters?

I posted a comment through my own Facebook, which attracted a lot of engagement and attention from my connections. I realized that this may be a wider conversation waiting to be had and so created a closed Facebook group, initially inviting only my connections. Once the conversations started, they then started inviting their friends and as such, it snowballed. The community grew organically.

How did you build your community and network?

At the start, my network mainly consisted of makeup artists and those in a similar field, due to my day job of being a makeup artist. Once I started Soul Sisters, the network started to grow as there was a common topic of interest and the private social setting welcomed everyday conversation. Due to the 'nothing is off topic' approach, womxn would join the group and start conversations, engage with comments and introduce themselves. Social media made it easy to reach a larger audience online and safely.

What were your fears when networking online?

Given our customer base, the areas of conversation are often taboo and customarily not welcomed in South Asian society, which is our core audience. Therefore, there are the obvious fears of where will this information go, who can see it, what will be done with it? However, I have worked very hard to keep it a trusted forum, leading decisions to decline troll accounts, block negative sentiments and audit those who enter. Despite the ample information now available on the internet, fears of networking online still come down to fake news and people. It is the responsibility of the organization and organizer to combat these and create comfort.

How has networking supported the growth of your business?

Having, creating and maintaining a network is fundamental to the birth and development of Soul Sisters. We wouldn't be here if it wasn't for the network. A simple example would be a few years ago, a close friend of the network shared the Facebook grant application and encouraged me to apply. Despite initially feeling like an imposter and as if we had nothing to offer, I sought help from the network on common grant mistakes and applied at the last minute. Literally, a few minutes before the deadline. I hadn't received the acceptance letter straight away as it had fallen into the spam folder, but once I had, it reaffirmed the need of this community as Facebook offered us one of their first community grants and a place on the programme! These funds helped me to create in-person events, the first season of our talk show, and to hire support staff to audit and grow the community group.

Why is forming and norming a sense of community so important?

Community is the foundation of what we do as human beings. To feel included, as if we belong and, most importantly, heard is the difference between having a life and living the life you want. The Soul Sisters group has helped women through difficult times, divorce, extramarital affairs, deaths, careers and loneliness. The norming of community is important as the 'old boys' network' exists to support men and so I wanted to disrupt that norm, to help women.

How did you transform from a Facebook group into a business?

It wasn't until a few years in I realized the power of this group! We started having businesses approach us in Pakistan to share product samples, talk to our members and get involved. Given the secrecy of the group, I didn't want to allow just anyone in. And so, I directed the conversations as new business opportunities, spoke to the marketing functions and secured what we felt were mutually beneficial engagements. For example, a leading Pakistani beauty brand paid me a set amount of money for permission to enter the group and provide free or discounted sample products to its members. The conversations were to be kept private and secure, though the data they collected was theirs to use. Eventually, other brands jumped on this approach and before I knew it, we had grown into a business model. It was then I had to seriously consider how I could take this full-time and turn it into a revenue-generating business.

How do you reach out to new connections?

It's funny because people think that I have someone working on my social media. I am my own brand and PR person. So with that being said, I constantly check my messages and reply to those who have messaged, as well as message others. I reach out to new connections in one of two ways: directly or through a mutual friend who can introduce me.

What are the struggles you've had?

Being a solo founder, you are responsible for the business, brand and by-product. In 2015 I was fighting the community fires within the groups while giving birth to my daughter. At that time, I realized the importance of the brand I was building as well as the responsibility it brings. I am constantly learning to be a better business owner, community builder and brand ambassador.

Top tips for new business founders?

Don't be afraid to start and go against the grain.

Afterthoughts

I admire the steps Kanwal has taken to bring taboo conversations to the table. These are topics that aren't often spoken about in South Asian communities. I have heard anecdotes of how her platform has positively benefited people who didn't otherwise have a space or security. She explains that building and listening to the community is a major reason why her business has bloomed. There's a reassuring element to her story – no one is prepared to be an entrepreneur and sometimes you don't even know there's a business opportunity. It often starts as an opportunity you need for yourself, and others end up joining.

Becoming an entrepreneur and launching my own business and brand online has been both scary and satisfying. It's amazing that an idea can change your life. The best part of this process has been my community, which includes supportive, thoughtful, brilliant people who are willing to extend a hand to help when I need it – and vice versa. Before I took the leap, I did suffer from loneliness, often comforting myself with Ben & Jerrys ice cream and R&B music. Now, I have a sense of community, a network of friends going through similar experiences, and the confidence to share my own insight. For anyone hesitant to start, remember that your experience is what can educate others, and is often what brings your business to life. Without my network or community, I wouldn't be half the entrepreneur I am today.

EXERCISE

In 2019, I created the 3-2-1 rule, a guide to establish networking confidence, build community support and practise your business introductions. I've turned it into a popular monthly challenge that many have found to be fruitful. Your task is to take on this challenge for six months and share your results on social media with the hashtag #321rule

---

Each month, you must do the following:

1 **Schedule a longer introduction call or coffee with one person** – consider sharing why you want a conversation, what benefit it will bring to you or the topic of discussion when sending this request.

2 **Connect with two of the three people on social media** – connecting means actively exchanging business details and following up.

3 **Start three conversations with three new people** – use the templates from this chapter, use webinar chats or ask your network for introductions.

Over the course of six months, you will have had 18 conversations; 18 new people will know about you and your business goals; you will have gained 12 new connections and have spoken to six people in depth about your business. By the end of this exercise, your circle will have expanded, your network will have grown and your community will be stronger!

WORKBOOK

_____

_____

_____

_____

_____

_____

_____

_____

_____

_____

_____

_____

_____

_____

_____

_____

_____

_____

_____

_____

_____

_____

_____

CHAPTER SIX

Does teamwork make the dream work?

Deciding to become an entrepreneur is the easy part. The difficulty arises when you're attempting to recruit employees and build a team.

In my case, I found that there are unique challenges that come with growing a team as a social entrepreneur. The mission of a social entrepreneur is focused on driving change towards a socially beneficial cause. However, more often than not, this mission does not lead to consistent income or donations, making it difficult to hire and pay staff.

Outside of the LMF Network, I was building my own business consultancy, including designing and delivering workshops on leadership, entrepreneurship and inclusive workplace cultures. In March 2020 I incorporated my consultancy as a limited company and in the same month, the LMF Network became a community interest company (CIC). Being the only permanent employee in both taught me the skills I had versus those that needed to be outsourced. It trained me to be considerate of people's needs when asking them to join, taking into account what they wanted and thinking deeply about how they could add value.

Growing a team is about involving people in your vision, allowing them to enhance it and develop it further.

Your business is your baby. Parting with control and delegating tasks to others is a challenge, one not often discussed within founder stories. I had a difficult time handing over the control of social media, newsletters and even workshops. Sometimes this was because I thought I knew best. At other times, it was because I hadn't quite communicated my vision to my teammates. In one instance, a team member sent me an ultimatum: either I let them have the autonomy or they'd leave.

Becoming a leader and growing your team comes with many difficult lessons. But once learnt, they can make you and your business more productive and more empathetic.

Time to grow your team

A few months into my entrepreneurial journey, I realized that I needed support. You aren't just a founder – you're also your own personal assistant, marketing manager, content creator, sales generator, financial controller, brand personality, network marketer, social media strategist, operations assistant and cheerleader.

That's a ton of roles and responsibilities! You need to grow your team because you're on the brink of burning out; you only have 24 hours in a day. Teamwork makes the dream work.

This next step in your entrepreneurial journey is about managing your workload, prioritizing your tasks and delegating the rest. Your team needs to believe in your vision and mission, but most importantly you. There is no product, service or output that is guaranteed to be successful. The road to success requires treating each member of your team as if they care as much about the business as you do – everyone is your stakeholder.

Didn't I tell you that there's a method to the entrepreneurial madness?

The future of work: functional and flexible

There are a few different ways to grow your team. The best advice I have been given is that working together is an extension of dating. Both parties must put in the time and effort to make things work – otherwise, the mismatch can lead to a fallout.

An **employee** is someone who is paid and works for a business over a substantial period of time. However, today, employees are less permanent and exist within a more malleable workplace. Flexible working allows employees to adapt their hours to their needs and deliverables. The UK Government website (Gov.uk, nd) outlines different types of flexible working arrangements, including:

- Role sharing – two people do one job and split the hours.
- Working remotely – completing the work from anywhere other than an employer's office.
- Flexitime – working the number of hours required around 'core hours' such as 10 am to 4 pm daily.

Sophie Smallwood, the co-founder of Roleshare, is a big advocate of sharing skills for jobs as a means to drive diversity, well-being and performance. She told me that flexible working 'allows for equal opportunities, fosters inclusion, and enables people to have a sustainable and fulfilling work–life balance'.

In my opinion, 2020 proved that flexible working is positive for businesses, allowing companies to hire a more international, diverse workforce, unrestricted by factors like geography and conventional work hours. Talented people exist around the world.

Before you start growing your team, take a moment to understand why –why you need them, why they should work with you and why this will be the best step for the business.

Seven ways to grow your team

A **volunteer** works within your business or organization in return for skill sharing and access to opportunities. Skill sharing is doing something you're good at in return for services you would otherwise have to pay for. This is a two-way trade, so you are asking for skills that you lack. For the LMF Network, we might bring on a volunteer to support digital marketing in return for help with presentation skills and CV writing. Often, volunteers are focused on gaining experience and the impact they'll create. Time commitments are usually dictated by the volunteer and should be managed with respect. Benefits to the business include understanding new perspectives, gaining support and trading skills.

An **apprentice** is contractually employed by your company and considered a full-time employee, with the benefits of pay, pension and annual leave. They will be employed and studying simultaneously to gain an external professional qualification. When hiring apprentices, ensure that they are treated as a member of the team with benefits. In the UK, businesses that want to hire apprentices need to be approved by the government scheme and must ensure they stick to regulatory procedures, as advised by the UK Government (Gov.uk, 2021). Benefits to you as an entrepreneur include gaining a new team member, teaching someone who is less experienced and gaining new perspectives.

A **contractor or freelancer** is someone who is employed on a fixed-term or project basis. They might have a portfolio career and hold a specific skill set. These types of roles can be filled by reaching out to your network, or using websites such as Fiverr or Freelance UK to find freelancers. In most instances, freelancers charge per hour and the platform takes a cut. Benefits to your business include working with people with a wide range of experiences and, in most cases, no need for extra team benefits such as insurance cover.

A **full-time employee** is someone who is employed by your business permanently until they either resign or are dismissed. They will likely have applied for the role, gone through a formal interview process and been offered permanent employment. Full-time employees require more benefits than the other options of staffing discussed so far, including pension plans, health care, statutory sick pay and a progression plan. Benefits to you include loyalty, long-term growth and the ability to delegate.

The next two types of employees we will discuss are those often associated with small business owners, especially if you are a solo entrepreneur.

A **co-founder** title exists to give equal credit to two people (or more) who start a business together. They may be part of the vision of a startup from the get-go, or they may be brought on very early by the original founder. They are likely to be someone who excels in a particular area of expertise that you are lacking and need support in. Unlike other employees, a co-founder is guaranteed shares or equity. At the start of LMF Network, the friend I messaged to attend networking events was the same friend who supported me in the idea to launch. Jui Joshi and I attended university together and had similar career ambitions, so I knew that she would believe in the vision. She was a serial entrepreneur and had successfully launched two businesses while working full time. At the start of our journey, Jui was what I would consider a co-founder; she supported all the plans, strategy and sales conversations. As we progressed as a community and eventually business, Jui progressed her co-founder status for a chair on the advisory board.

An **advisory board** provides non-binding strategic advice to the management of your business. The informal nature of an advisory board gives greater flexibility in structure and management compared to the board of directors. The process of finding advisors differs across businesses. Best practice would encourage you to have a job-like description of the tasks expected from an advisor, predicted meeting times, the level of involvement in decisions and what they would receive from the arrangement. An advisory board is a non-paying binding relationship in most cases.

The final method to grow your team is one that happened to be the most important decision in growing my business model, brand and community.

A **franchise** is loosely defined as the letting of a business, brand or name. I use the word 'loosely' because a traditional franchise is a method of distributing business and establishing a brand presence through a lawful contract binding two parties with initial fees, royalties and rights. However, with the LMF Network, I helped our Toronto chapter founder Beenish Saeed create a franchise with a contract that I wrote and had checked by lawyers in our network. It's worth considering the franchise model if you want to expand your business or, equally, bring in another person to run their own branch. Benefits of franchising include being a part of something bigger, experiencing entrepreneurship while being supported by a model or brand that already exists and therefore its learnings, and still being able to exercise creative freedom.

My experience of growing the team

As with anything, growing a team is a learning process. Below are three examples of where I grew my team.

Growing the advisory board

In 2019, we identified that our skills gap could be filled with an advisory board composed of individuals who were more experienced in business growth.

What steps were taken?

- **Information gathering through our network** – initially, I reached out to my network on LinkedIn and read materials easily available online to learn more about how advisory boards were typically chosen and structured.

- **Identifying roles and creating job descriptions** – I adapted three job descriptions to suit the needs of my business and shared these on LinkedIn, which was the social platform I engaged with most. There was no payment for these roles other than covering travel and expenses. All roles were formed to complement my skills and bring a direction into the business.
- **Interviewing potential candidates** – within one week, we had received 30 applications, far more than expected! All applications were screened and interviewed. To ensure a fair process, the interviews were summarized in a Google document and each interviewee scored out of five on five main areas: passion, experience, expertise, skills and social commitment.

In September 2019, we announced our first three advisors and they stayed with us for 18 months.

ON REFLECTION

I found having an advisory board difficult, because at times I was unsure what to send their way. I felt like I was burdening them and focused on sharing results rather than involving them in the building effort. At the end of 2021, our advisory board had stepped down, as they'd served for 18 months and it was time for a refresh. I took their feedback on board and used this to better my relationships with team members. Their advice was simply, 'leaders must communicate, schedule regular meetings and have areas where they need help'. In hindsight, I went into having an advisory board earlier than I should have because I felt stuck. It's best to consider an advisory board once you have established the business's foundation and identified gaps that they can support.

Growing the franchise

In 2019, Beenish Saeed approached us through a mutual friend. She expressed her interest in making the community international.

What steps were taken?

- **Introduction conversations** – at the start, Beenish and I would speak regularly on the phone discussing our intentions, ideas and visions. This was an exercise for both of us to understand the other's motivations and if we could work together.
- **Discussion with the advisory board** – the plans and motivations were presented to advisors, who were able to provide their knowledge and expertise, while asking the relevant questions that sometimes get overlooked by excited founders.
- **Contract creation and agreement** – because I had no education in law, I reached out to friends of the network and asked for support to create a contract outlining expectations, terms and conditions. This was shared with Beenish to check over and agree on.

In January 2020, LMF Toronto soft-launched and Beenish led the mission as our first chapter founder outside the UK. Since its launch, Beenish has grown the brand, onboarded volunteers, worked with companies such as Catalyst and General Assembly, and overseen the launch of LMF Queen's, our first university society. The LMF Queen's University Society was founded by Shanzeh Chaudry, a chemistry student, who wanted to bridge the knowledge gap between women studying STEM and how students enter the corporate world. She shares that 'as our university life and normalcy was disrupted with COVID-19, the need to connect and engage with other students became more evident. LMF provided a community of role models, education around career options and inspiration that things can get better. I hoped to provide the same opportunity for my peers at Queen's University.'

ON REFLECTION

I thought that running a franchise model would be smooth sailing. However, what I didn't consider was how to resolve conflict, stay transparent when business was moving so fast and maintain motivation. There were a number of instances where Beenish and I had differing views. As a founder, I thought I had a right to make the decision. However, given that our values were formed with community and collaboration in mind, I had to step away from my ego and invite another opinion. Beenish was passionate, complemented my skill set and had the geographical knowledge that I didn't have. Small businesses that franchise must be prepared for a teething period with discussions around brand assets, logos, communication styles and services. For example, when LMF Toronto grew towards running diversity workshops, it was time for us to go back to the contract and make amends.

Growing the volunteers

Once we decided to launch the network as a social enterprise, it was time to expand the team. From past experience with volunteers, I found that the optimum time for a volunteer or intern to stay before heading on to pastures new was three months. This time period was derived from an analysis of what worked for our organization, especially as many were skill swapping or learning new skills on the job.

What steps were taken?

- **Identifying roles and creating job descriptions** – for each area of support, including marketing, project management and operations, I researched the typical job descriptions available on the market and adapted these to suit the needs of our business. These were no more than a few sentences for each. We shared these opportunities on LinkedIn, Instagram and Twitter with an email address to contact.
- **Interviewing potential volunteers** – within one day, we had received 30 applications via email with CVs attached. I arranged interview slots via our Calendly link and shared these with potential candidates to book in.
- **Flexible contracts and value establishment** – over the course of three weeks, I spoke to 30+ people, understanding their motives, establishing connections and asking how we could compensate them outside of money.

At the start of 2021, we onboarded three interns to handle operations, marketing and PR. Despite not having immediate funds, I was able to reimburse them with the minimum wage for their time and support them in achieving the goals we'd agreed upon.

ON REFLECTION

Inviting volunteers and interns into the business has been exceptionally rewarding. I have been able to learn from new perspectives and ways of doing things, while enabling volunteers to achieve their goals. However, areas that I didn't account for included a rigorous onboarding session, performance reviews and regular catch-ups. Onboarding is crucial as it provides a common understanding of the business, introductions to other team members, and invites to software or tools used. Regularly tracking someone's confidence and capability at the start of their working life enables you to see their progression, or lack of it.

Skill sharing and skill swapping are core to the future of working because they allow individuals to test if that's what they actually want to do before committing to it. For example, one volunteer stepped in to manage our website. Three months later, she realized she hated working in website and UX design but enjoyed content creation. This new-found passion has taken her from technology to film production and design.

Running a team also requires maintaining motivation, managing progress and focusing on your vision. There are moments when this won't happen, or your team members' output won't be satisfactory. Managing difficult conversations is a skill every leader must learn.

As a founder, I recall letting my emotions drive the conversation, rather than logic. When handling a difficult conversation, it's important to understand what your ideal outcome is, be open to data points or evidence, and enable two-way conversations. Especially when team members are less experienced, it's worth considering that they may need more time to absorb and dissect information, feedback or concerns.

Gabriela Hersham, the founder of Huckletree, told me over an Instagram Live that during the Covid-19 pandemic she had to 'reduce the size of her team by 50 per cent' and as such the conversations were 'extremely difficult and very candid'. Entrepreneurship is a bumpy road – in the less-good times, 'it's the responsibility of the leaders themselves to take accountability and to share bad news in a candid, transparent way'. Gabriela went on to share that in her experience, she feels comfortable delegating high-impact tasks to other team members as she is 'certain that we are all aligned in terms of our vision for the business and the values which are going to direct how we get there. When you have high levels of alignment, you don't need to direct your team members to a certain point – you provide as much context as you can but you empower them, as the experts in their fields, to make all key decisions.'

Let's grow your team!

In Table 6.1, I have allocated five columns to help lay out a plan for who you might need to hire and what skills are required.

- Next 18 months' goals – what are you wanting to achieve in the next 18 months with clear deliverables?
- What can you do/do you have? A list of skills or resources you have available or have access to.
- What you need/can't do – a list of skills or resources you would like to have access to.
- Summarize into skills – outline the exact skills you're looking for from a person.
- Who do we need? Summarize the task in a job title or something similar, which equates to the heading of the job advert or ask.

TABLE 6.1   How to grow your team

Next 18 months' goals	What can you do/do you have?	What you need/can't do	Summarize into skills	Who do we need?
Gain £20K in charity funding	Network of people Access to funding portals	Time for applications Grant writing background	Grant writing Fundraising Understanding of terminology	Fundraising associate or grant writer
Design and deliver four life skills programmes virtually	Understanding of topics wanted	Time to organize events, send comms and follow up marketing	Operations Project management for virtual events Marketing experience	Events and operations executive

Can your team find you?

Now that you have identified who you are looking for and why, it's time to create a job advert. As a new business owner, you most likely don't have the resources to work with top recruitment firms or boost job posts. I don't think they're necessary. Traditional routes to employment are no longer the only avenues available today. In order to ensure diverse applications, colleagues and teams, we must ensure that our hiring practice is also diverse, inclusive and equitable.

A study carried out by Boston Consulting Group in 2018 found that diverse teams can increase company profitability by 19 per cent (Lorenzo *et al*, 2018). Similar results were shared by McKinsey & Company in 2018, who stated that diverse teams can increase productivity by 33 per cent (Hunt *et al*, 2018). If none of the other reasons resonate, then these studies have compelling evidence from a purely financial standpoint. Diversity needs to be at the forefront of entrepreneurs' minds as they launch and grow their businesses.

Some methods to find your team include:

- reaching out to your network;
- sharing job postings on diverse community platforms or social media;
- working with universities and educational institutions;
- partnering with or participating in an accelerator/incubator programme.

A good job description is essential for a good team member

A job description describes the tasks, expectations and duties of the position. This is for the benefit of the company as much as for your future colleague. Research shows shorter job descriptions received 8.4 per cent more applications and most people spend 14 seconds deciding if they want to apply or not (McLaren, 2019).

How to write a job description

There is no right or wrong job description, only clear or confusing.

Let's make a good job description:

- **Introduce the business** – a short summary of the business, outlining your story, successes and future plans.
- **Job summary** – a few sentences to summarize the ask, expectations and future scope of the role.
- **Job responsibilities** – keep these to a maximum of five, clearly outlined with clear deliverables.
- **Job qualifications** – keep these to a maximum of five points and limited to things you definitely require, not ones that are nice to have.
- **Benefits** – a few sentences or bullet points listing what the business is offering, such as remote working, access to technology, skill sharing, lunch, etc.

- **Contact information** – clear links to how to apply and where to find more information, and links to your social platforms.
- **Next steps** – share the expected time of reply, when interviews are taking place and what someone can expect from the process.

All language in job descriptions should be gender-neutral, inviting anyone to apply. Gendered terms are part of the language that are subtly gender-coded; society has certain expectations of what men and women are like, and this seeps into the language we use. This negatively impacts motivations to apply, the number of candidates interested, and limits inclusion. Some gendered terms include 'bossy', 'dominant' or 'competitive'. My advice would be to sense-check your work; ask your team to be a second pair of eyes before any job descriptions go outside and use online plugin tools such as Grammarly for extra support.

How do you filter candidates and conduct an interview?

The task of interviewing and filtering candidates can be exhausting. Remember to schedule interviews within an allocated time frame, use free tools such as Google Sheets to take notes, and go into interviews with a scorecard. Remember, people make the company. Frame your questions around your business values to understand if potential candidates align with your wider vision.

I often find organizations wanting to hire for culture fit, hoping that someone can smoothly merge with existing colleagues. However, this approach can influence you into hiring people who look and feel the same, limiting the diversity of perspectives and experiences on your team.

WHAT ARE SOME THINGS YOU CAN DO TO ENSURE FAIR RECRUITMENT?

- **Prepare a consistent assessment** – unconscious biases are the social beliefs held about a certain group of people that one forms without realizing. For example, favouring a candidate with a bachelor's degree and no experience over someone who has experience but no degree. Or, assuming that a woman wants kids, especially when engaged or married. Or, someone with an 'English' name being more likely to understand the market and perform better, than one without. Ensure that as an interviewer, you are being fair in your judgement, asking the same questions and eliminating unconscious biases.

- **Leave time for questions** – invite candidates to ask more about the business, role and future.
- **Invite diverse interviewers to join** – if you already have an advisory board, colleagues or partners for your business, ask them if they can sit in the interview with you, or to talk through the filtered candidates who you think fit the bill.
- **Feedback** – follow up with emails and next steps. Even if someone wasn't able to go through the next round, send them feedback. Consider the time spent applying and researching for the interview – the least you can do is ensure fair feedback. This will ensure you leave the conversation on good terms and support someone in their development.

As a small business owner, you won't have time to conduct several interviews per person, especially if the roles you are recruiting for are voluntary or short placements. I would recommend sticking to two interview rounds, conducted within a short time frame.

Why is diverse and inclusive recruitment important to growing your business and team?

Diversity and inclusion recognize that people are different and their experiences unique. This is important to allow people to thrive, without the need to conform or change who they are.

Verna Myers, the head of diversity and inclusion for Netflix, famously said 'Diversity is being invited to the party. Inclusion is being asked to dance' (Sherbin and Rashid, 2017).

Figure 6.1 is built on her work, which I have developed further:

- Diversity is being 'invited to the party'.
- Inclusion is 'having the music to dance to'.
- Equity is 'being able to dance without any barriers'.

These three pillars build a strong foundation for belonging and help create a healthy working environment.

As a corporate employee, I had the misfortune of feeling like I didn't belong. I even ended up leaving two employers before my contract ended. I entered the workplace with high hopes and was disheartened by the lack of investment they placed in their people. Additionally, the education around diversity and inclusion was limited.

FIGURE 6.1   Diversity, inclusion and equity

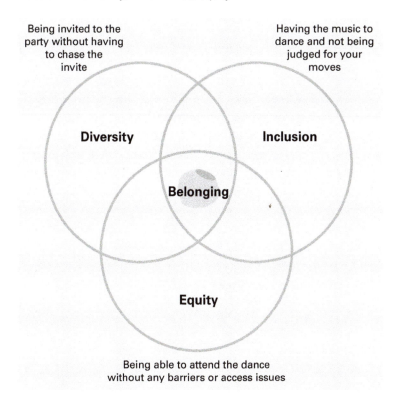

115

To understand the knowledge around diversity and inclusion, the LMF Network conducted research and released their initial report in 2021 (Khan and Barlow, 2021). We found that 'less than 50 per cent of people know how diversity and inclusion impact their daily lives' and '78 per cent of employees believe that their company's diversity and inclusion initiatives are to tick a box, rather than create real change'.

It's imperative to your business as a whole that you establish pure practices from the foundation up. An analogy I often use is 'ensure the foundations of your house are strong before you invite others for tea'. If you want to learn more about diversity, inclusion and equity in the business, please feel free to reach out or connect with me via my website, where I have further resources available.

Five things to consider when growing your business and team

Here are some other things to consider:

1 When growing your team, remember that all practices should be contractual and abide by deliverables.
2 Performance reviews should be regular, with discussions around salary, responsibilities and progression.
3 Rotational short stints for interns and volunteers work better than longer ones and encourage evolving roles and improving skills.
4 Share regular business updates and invite employees into discussions. It can be demotivating if you are sending out orders but never allowing for open communication.
5 Don't be afraid to pause hiring if it doesn't feel right or you feel you're not giving it your best.

If you are struggling with any of the areas covered in this chapter, lean on your community. Feel free to get in touch with me and I can invite you to the LMF Network Slack community.

Handing over control of your business may be a difficult task but one that you must consider. Business owners think they are interchangeable with their business – this isn't true, whether it's your first or fifth business. Growing my team has been the best thing to happen to my business. I have been challenged, changed perspectives and added in team members who see my vision as an extension of themselves. Give team members the time to explore all options and invite them to bring their own perspective. Your team will work wonders if you are able to truly invest in their learning, potential and leadership.

CASE STUDY   Beenish Saeed

Beenish Saeed is a Pakistani author, an award-winning speaker and the franchise founder of LMF Toronto. She founded the chapter in late 2019, launching it in early 2020 as the first chapter of LMF Network outside the UK. Beenish has lived and worked in eight cities across Europe, North America and Asia, driving her work in social, technological and legal impact.

Why did you decide to launch LMF in Toronto?

I've always believed that inclusion is a growth strategy. This belief motivated the launch of LMF in Toronto, as I saw a two-fold Canadian socioeconomic problem as a first-generation immigrant: for a country that prides itself on its liberal immigration policies, Canada needs to do a lot of work for its job markets. Around 300,000 new immigrants move to Canada every year, mostly through skilled work and education streams. They are mostly unemployed due to a lack of 'Canadian' work experience. With an ageing population, Canada could see huge immigration debts in the future, if adequate employment support is not provided to incoming immigrants. Secondly, for residents under the age of 30, it's a struggle to build experience in the field they have trained for, in order to pursue employment. LMF Toronto focuses on providing networks to make the right connections, learn winning skills that reduce the length of the job search process and letting individuals gain Canadian work experience with authenticity.

Has it been hard working with a team remotely and, if so, what have you put in place to overcome those challenges?

Working remotely has allowed us to fail fast and learn fast, to arrive at a simple formula:

Multiple Technology Options + Emotional Support & Encouragement = Happy Remote Teams

I could have mentioned 'Successful' instead of 'Happy' in the formula, but happiness of teams comes first to me, especially when you are collaborating on an intentional cause of advancing marginalized communities. We use emails, calls, text messaging and Slack messaging to structure our meetings and keep in touch. We talk more, ask for help and act as a group of friends, since we are all entrepreneurial. As we grow, I plan to incorporate happiness metrics to understand the well-being of our team and create a compensation plan for all of us. Supportive engagements go a long way in motivating us to collaborate on worldwide campaigns and design economically effective skills workshops.

How did you find, recruit and retain team members for your business?

LMF Toronto, at its inception, was a lean organization as it was led by myself. Just two months into this endeavour, I delivered our first LinkedIn success workshop, which hosted around 2,000 attendees and became one of our most successful events. Spreading our footprint among nearly 200 North American cities via that single workshop was a milestone. The heartwarming messages and LinkedIn requests were great, but what sweetened the deal was when I received emails from three wonderful women, who were inspired to join me. These same women became our first LMF Toronto volunteers.

Retaining the team is a combination of listening, learning and leading. Listening to what they want and how you can help them; learning about the various perspectives they bring into the business and leading the business (and the team) strategically to meet our KPIs.

Our process was not formal but structured. The team have creative freedom and as a result, I have enjoyed how entrepreneurial and risk-taking we are. We took the time to understand one another and accommodate each other with honesty and encouragement. We believe that sustaining our relationships is a marathon and not a sprint. Our mutual interest to integrate (and not segregate) was extremely convincing and I can proudly say I was not wrong in trusting them.

What are some benefits you have found expanding and founding a brand that was trying to establish itself in a different location?

Founding and growing LMF in Toronto has been experimental, complex and even frustrating, but the drive to achieve repeatability in a different location helps us take advantage of learning-curve effects. London, in comparison to Toronto, has hundreds of companies with active on-the-job training and inclusion programmes. We quickly understood that while inclusion is not a taboo topic in Toronto, it is seen as a cost centre by most businesses, except for legacy non-profit organizations, which are widely connected with corporate Canada. The world of high-growth startups in Toronto still has a long way to go.

The example of Nike, which branched out from shoes to balls, equipment and golf apparel, hits close to home. We've altered our approach from our core chapter's, to arrive at the best formula of repeatability. We've also analysed the best avenues to reach a high number of people in need of career help, so by changing one thing at a time we have made adjacency moves to increase our footprint without straining our entire collective. We are creating a new CEO School series, to train the next generation of C-suite executives to communicate effectively to diverse communities of consumers and get comfortable with talking about shifting cultural demographics. We are also uniquely positioned to conduct immigrant-specific research in a cosmopolitan city like Toronto, as we have received positive support towards our Immigrant Mindset campaigns, which are hugely inspired by Cuban-American entrepreneur, speaker and bestselling author, Glenn Llopis. As we improve this, our speed and strategic clarity will elevate with the help of our endorsers in Canadian communities

Afterthoughts

Working with Beenish and growing the team has made me a better leader, as I have understood the importance of sharing the workload, asking for help and seeking new perspectives. Initially, when I launched LMF Network, all big decisions were dictated by me. It limited our progress. Beenish coming on to the team pushed me to change. Beenish led several new services that were not available in the UK, and I had to believe that she knew best what would work for her market. At first I was defensive, but soon realized that inclusion is important for all verticals. Eventually, I came to realize that I had to give direction and trust my colleagues to lead the way. The business would not have flourished if the team had not grown. Yes, it was hard to give up control, but there is no risk without reward.

WORKBOOK

_____

_____

_____

_____

_____

_____

_____

_____

_____

_____

_____

_____

_____

_____

_____

_____

_____

_____

_____

_____

_____

_____

_____

_____

_____

_____

CHAPTER SEVEN

The three Ps of leadership: people, power and purpose

I have often been told I have a memorable presence. I have bumped into people 20 years on who remember me from a classroom, from an interaction at a store or from a conversation we once had. My personality has always been joyful, animated and competitive. I am the kind of person who will challenge myself to see if I can achieve something, just to see if it's possible. However, somewhere between university and my first few corporate jobs, I lost my sense of self and conformed to someone else's version of me. I became unsure of myself and lacked a sense of identity.

Once I left the corporate world to start my business, I realized that I had the freedom to be myself and explore my own style of leadership. I also realized that the leadership styles I had previously seen around me didn't suit my personality – they didn't inspire me to be better or work harder. I was essentially only turning up for the paycheck. I have had leaders who have not inspired me, told me I wasn't good enough despite hiring me and constantly put down my ideas only to resurface them as their own in meetings.

Since becoming a leader in my business, I have embraced my personality and continuously worked on becoming better daily. I ask my colleagues to challenge me, bring the team into strategic discussions and send regular updates so they know what's happening behind the scenes. The reason my business has flourished is that I allow myself to be authentic. I share the good, bad and ugly, and the wins and struggles. I am a firm believer that people buy into people. The question is – who are you?

This question will help you become a better leader and will teach you how to embrace the three Ps of leadership: people, power and purpose. We will establish how to overcome imposter syndrome, and build your brand online using LinkedIn as our tool of choice.

What is leadership?

In a 2020 *Medium* article, author Jacob Morgan writes that he interviewed a number of leaders to ask their definition of 'leadership'. In most cases, he was greeted by an awkward pause. He quotes Marissa Mayer, Former CEO of Yahoo!, and her definition was 'leadership is helping believe in a better tomorrow or a better outcome than you have today', in contrast to Ajay Banga, the CEO of Mastercard, who suggests 'a leader is someone who can think strategically, simplify the strategy so everyone in the organization can understand it and communicate that strategy simply, enthusiastically, and in a caring way'. To me, being a leader isn't necessarily about having direct reports beneath you. Being a leader for your business is being a public driver for its growth, being the face of it and the person that embodies its vision. When your team grows, being a leader is also how you direct others to serve that mission, but you don't have to have employees to secure your boss status!

Growing up in South Asian culture, leadership was often associated with those who were older. I was never told what characteristics a leader must have but those who were older were automatically given a title: 'aunty' or 'uncle' or *'bhai'* or *'baji'*, meaning brother or sister, and should be respected. This meant no answering back, no eye contact, and not calling them by their first name. To respect a leader, one must not challenge their views but simply say *'jee'* (yes) and walk away.

Being raised this way, I initially found it difficult to raise concerns or have heated conversations with senior stakeholders in a corporate setting. I would often look down at their collar rather than into their eyes, which didn't make me look very confident, though it was a sign of respect where I came from.

In hindsight, it was these same leaders who turned out to be awful managers, with no cross-cultural knowledge and little understanding of how to motivate their employees. A good leader proactively coaches themselves to better their people, inspire others with the purpose of their organization and understand where their employees are coming from. Since running my startup and becoming my own boss, I have separated leadership from age or experience, and defined it as the ability to guide, influence and motivate others.

What type of leader are you?

The first step to deciding the type of leader you would like to be is pinpointing the leaders who have impacted your life.

In 2021, as I reflected on the year that had passed, I wrote a blog on LinkedIn titled 'Bad vibes don't make healthy lives'. I argued that my experiences with bad leadership were the motivation for me to become a good leader. Bad leadership may be someone who doesn't encourage or grow your strengths, is often putting you down or doesn't enable you to grow. In contrast, many of my successes have been because of good leaders supporting me. These leaders were real allies, putting in the work to ensure their social power could help to elevate me where possible. I defined positive leadership traits like empathy, honesty and championing, inspired by teachers, supervisors and friends.

Self-reflection is a key trait when becoming a leader. It can mean the difference between leaders who simply lead and leaders who influence, encourage and motivate others to believe in their mission.

The four types of leadership personalities

Do you consider yourself competitive or compassionate? An influencer or someone easily influenced? Before heading into the styles of leadership, let's take a moment to learn about the personality styles that exist innately within us.

A personality style is an individual's consistent characteristics and preferences across contexts. Your personality is the dynamic personal traits and patterns of behaviour that are unique to yourself.

One of the most famous corporate personality style tests is DiSC (DiSC nd).

DiSC® is a personal assessment tool used to improve teamwork, communication and productivity. It was adapted from a concept created by William Moulton Marston in 1928. From his research, Marston categorized a person's perception of self in relationship to their environment using four labels:

- Dominance (D) – direct, dominating, driven, strong willed.
- Inducement (I) – influencing, interactive, lively, talkative.
- Submission (S) – steady, accommodating, considerate, patient.
- Compliance (C) – cautious, disciplined, critical, questioning.

Though this style of the test has been proven to not be a representative assessment in the long term, as people's style and personality adapt over time, it does provide an understanding of your baseline personality traits. Since its conception in 1928, the model has been revisited and evolved.

When I deliver workshops and training for leaders or aspiring leaders, I ask them to take a moment to reflect on these categories and identify where they think they fit best. This is a gut reaction, not a certified test result.

Using your gut instinct, which DISC characteristic takes priority in your decisions in the following scenarios?

1 You are renegotiating your contract with a client in an international location.
2 Your team member schedules a meeting in your calendar to discuss promotion and pay.
3 Your colleague suggests that they are having a tough time on social media due to heightened anxiety, despite this being a big part of their daily tasks.

There is no right or wrong with the answers or your approach as a leader. As an entrepreneur, before you know it you will be considered a leader and so it's important to know the kind of leader you want to actively become. One method of understanding your leadership style is to ask your colleagues, friends and business partners for any feedback they may be able to provide. 360-degree feedback is feedback gathered from a number of people, to provide a holistic view of who you are and how you are perceived by others. After receiving this feedback, take a moment to reflect on the information and identify areas to continue improving. Align this feedback with your business goals, prioritize your leadership style and go grow your business!

Are leaders born or made?

A ResearchGate (2017) discussion among academics concludes that there is no single answer. Kirkpatrick and Locke (1991) believe that 'the possession of certain traits alone does not guarantee leadership success' but there is evidence that effective leaders are different from other people in certain key respects. They found that key leader traits include: 'drive, motivation, honesty, cognitive ability; and knowledge of the business'. On the other hand, research by Black *et al* (1999) suggests that 'leaders are born and then made'. From their findings, they state that your impact and ability as a leader come from 'being competent and interested; someone who is always pushing frontiers, challenging the status quo and presenting the bigger picture'.

There may be people around you, including yourself, who naturally feel more comfortable leading, influencing and sharing. In my opinion, this only means that you have the foundation for what it takes to become a good leader. After running my own business and building a brand, I believe that everyone should take leadership training, leaders should not be promoted without training, and leadership training modules should be delivered in schools. We become leaders and adapt our styles from a young age, and it's a shame we don't nurture these skill sets.

Here are six types of leadership styles, which I have seen around me:

An **authoritative leader** imposes expectations and defines outcomes. This style of leadership focuses on rules, processes and structure. Although this is an effective style of leadership, reducing time on crucial decisions and emphasizing the chain of command, it can also limit creativity and collaboration.

A **participative leader** is rooted in bringing people together to make a collective decision. This style of leadership prefers to include team members in all decisions and as such, teams are normally stronger and motivated. However, this can also mean the decision-making process itself is time-consuming and can delay outcomes.

A **delegative leader** is one who focuses on delegating initiatives and tasks to team members. This style of leader prefers to build on team creativity and take advantage of experience. However, this style can also bring difficulties when adapting to change and bring an additional layer of work when creating clear command and communication structures.

A **transactional leader** is one who is seen to deliver give and take. This style of leader creates specific time-bound goals that are achievable, creates a clear communication chain and encourages employees to choose reward systems. However, this style can also limit innovation and be seen to consider employees as followers, rather than enhance their leadership qualities.

A **transformational leader** is one who inspires followers or community with a vision and empowers them to achieve it. This style of leadership focuses on placing a high value on vision, gaining the trust of followers by motivating them to use their past experiences, and encourages their input. However, this style can also deviate from the protocols and requires consistent feedback from colleagues or community.

A **coaching leader** is one who identifies the individual strengths of each member and nurtures them. This style of leader focuses on strategies to enable their team to work better alone and together. This can be done through aligning skills with tasks, ensuring diversity of members to complement one another and constant feedback. However, this style can also be very time-consuming, hard to manage especially if you're growing quickly and may mean that at some time, certain skills are no longer required within the business.

Your leadership style will adapt and shift depending on your situation and circumstances. Some people will find leadership easier given their personality and communication style; others may shy away from tasks due to their own reservations.

Chief Client Officer at OMD Jess Roberts defines a leader as 'someone who empowers others to be the best they can be, able to unlock potential in everyone. One who has empathy, listens well and is able to build diverse high-performing teams that create value.' Jess leads hundreds of people across EMEA and handles the relationships with business clients. I ask her how leaders who manage remote teams can empower others to do their best, to which she replies 'finding ways to give them a voice that doesn't rely on them speaking up on a Zoom call, sharing content for feedback at people's own pace and creating more space for one-on-one conversations to get their point of view'. Having started my passion project while in full-time employment, I know first-hand how businesses aren't ready to support their people in launching entrepreneurial ideas, which could result in losing great talent. Jess echoes this sentiment and explains that in her opinion, 'it's important we create space for people to grow, and this includes supporting side hustles, which are often in areas they are passionate about. Giving people time in the working week to get away from emails and meetings to spend time on personal development and growth. If the organization can support the side hustle and encourage a colleague to follow their business dreams, then it can only benefit the organization to help build the skills and strengths of this individual, which will inevitably be translated back into the office environment.' Jess's comments echo my own thoughts – leadership isn't about providing a certain response in a given situation, but about fine-tuning your authentic strengths to inspire, motivate and empower others. As an entrepreneur, like a manager, you're not given a handbook on how to be a good leader. It's an iterative process that evolves as you build.

Get to know your team members

As a leader, one of the best pieces of advice I have received is to create a cheat sheet.

A leading startup founder shared that each time she has a new joiner, she asks them to create a short 'ways of working' document, which can be shared with the other team members. This allows for this particular person to feel involved, while enabling leaders to best inspire their team.

Here's an example version:

My name is _____
I identify as _____
My core working hours are _____
I prefer to work in the following ways:

1 _____

2 _____

3 _____

When sending me an email, I prefer the following _____
When working towards a deadline, please indicate _____
If you see me _____ please know that I am actually _____
If you want to discuss ways of working outside of this, please
    contact me directly via _____, my working hours are _____ and
    I prefer a _____-minute meeting scheduled directly into my
    calendar with clear agenda points.

There are moments when you may doubt yourself and your ability. This exercise is great for you to identify how you work best, which working environment fuels your growth and how you can make the best use of your time. Communicating with your colleagues to ensure you understand how to best support them can be the difference between a creative and inclusive culture where people can thrive, or one where people suffer.

Leaders aren't meant to have it all under control but can find methods to create impact and efficiencies. There are times where you may feel down or in doubt about your leadership skills, but that is very natural.

Do you ever feel like you don't deserve the gold star?

In primary school, students are often presented with gold stars as rewards if they get something correct, contribute to the class or show initiative. A gold star is easily perceived to be an award for doing something 'right'. Yet, over time, we seem to pick up on a feeling that we don't deserve these gold stars.

Many of us today have moments where we consider ourselves undeserving of our accolades. You might convince yourself that it wasn't even you who completed the task or that you didn't deserve the full credit.

Within the first two years of building my business, I constantly felt like an imposter. When I was presented with an award, I would list five other people who deserved it more; when someone showed up for my workshops, I'd be shocked, thinking no one would be interested. The LMF Network community has grown from an idea I had, and yet there are moments I have to remind myself that this idea was my own. The recognition others provide is never enough to match the recognition you need from yourself.

When my publisher confirmed this book was a go-ahead, I felt like an imposter each time I sat down to write. I realized I was trying to be someone else – I am not a writer, and they didn't want a writer – they wanted a real person with lived experience to share their story. If you feel like an imposter, then you are in good company. So do some of the smartest minds – up to 70 per cent of people experience imposter-like feelings at some point (Sakulku and Alexander, 2011).

What is imposter syndrome?

Imposter syndrome is the idea that you have succeeded or earned your stripes because of luck and not qualifications. This concept was first identified by psychologists Pauline Rose Clance and

Suzanne Imes in 1978 (Templar, 2021). It's the feeling of not being enough, feeling like you haven't achieved anything and constantly doubting yourself. An example of this is when you have interviewed for a job role and made it to the third round, negotiated your salary and still, within the first week of being there, you think you shouldn't have been hired because those around you are smarter, more capable or more qualified.

Some things you may think when feeling like an imposter:

- I don't think I deserve the successes I have obtained.
- I feel like a fraud.
- I find it difficult to accept compliments.

The five types of imposter syndrome

The **perfectionist** sets excessively high goals for themselves and when they fail to reach these, they experience self-doubt and worry. This type of imposter can also be more controlling and will tend to carry out tasks on their own. This style of imposter must learn to take mistakes in their stride. There is never a 'perfect time' to start your work and mistakes are inevitable.

The **superperson** feels that they are lesser compared to their colleagues or counterparts and so work harder to measure up. This may mean staying in the office longer, checking emails at odd times of the day or being deemed a workaholic. This style of imposter must learn to compliment themselves rather than look for external validation, nurture inner confidence and take criticism constructively not personally.

The **natural genius** feels that they are naturally good at something and so if something takes longer to master, it can cause adverse feelings. This type of imposter sets their bar very high and then judges themselves on the number of attempts taken to complete a task. This style of imposter must learn to see themselves as a work in progress, honing impactful skills and realigning tasks to strengths.

The **soloist** is someone who would rather do the task themselves, as asking for help can result in having to prove their worth or being found out as a fraud. This type of imposter believes that they can do everything alone. This style of imposter must learn to include people in the process and learn that it's okay to ask for help.

The **expert** is someone who measures their competence based on what and how much they know or can do. This type of imposter feels that they will never know enough and therefore fear being exposed as unknowledgeable. This style of imposter must learn to learn skills when required rather than hoarding knowledge, remind themselves that tasks will change, as will the traits required, and can take on extra responsibilities such as mentoring or volunteering, to share knowledge with others and also to learn.

No matter the profile you think defines you, struggling with self-confidence is a feeling I believe that everyone has felt at least once in their life – so you aren't alone.

Mamta Gera, a leadership coach and consultant, has recognized imposter syndrome in many of her clients and works with them to overcome it. Mamta shares that the 'impact of imposter syndrome is significant. It prevents leaders from applying for promotions, speaking up in meetings and making positive changes (such as changing jobs or starting a new business).' Mamta believes the first step in managing this is to 'have self-awareness. Awareness of the type of imposter syndrome you may have and what situations trigger it are important. Once you are aware, you can change and manage it. This can either be through techniques like self-distancing and expressive writing, or seeking further help such as coaching.' Coaching is a practice where a more experienced or trained professional supports you in improving your performance. Having recognized the impact imposter syndrome has on her clients, Mamta created a global course on Skillshare to positively impact as many people as possible and help them to fulfil their potential.

The three Ss to overcome imposter syndrome

As the leader, people are looking to you for advice, focus and direction. This doesn't mean you can't have bad days.

If most of us feel like imposters, how do we fix it?

2019 was my year of strategically winging it and challenging myself to grow. However, the more times I said yes, the noisier my life became. According to my mentor, I was saying yes to everything and my personal mission was getting diluted. As a result of this conversation, I developed the three Ss – a simple yet effective way to realign your strengths and skills, and remind you of the impact you have created.

EXERCISE

1 *Skills or strengths – Skills and strengths* – write a list of all the skills and strengths that you believe you have.

2 *Success story* – for each trait identified, note down a story of when you used this skill or strength successfully.

3 *So what?* – For each success story, note down its impact or the result that was driven by it.

I encourage you to do this exercise on a regular basis. Update this document constantly and think of it as your personal CV or tracker. Refer back to this document when you're having a bad day or you need a little pick me up before you go into business meetings!

Building your boss brand online

It's time to use all this information to build your brand. In previous chapters, we have discussed branding for your business. Now it's branding for you – the boss!

Your personal brand is the combination of skills and experiences that make you who you are. It's how you present yourself, what makes you different and why someone should trust you. Jeff Bezos, the founder of Amazon, is famously alleged to have said that your personal brand is 'what people say about you when you are not in the room'.

Remember, people buy into people. To grow your business, your brand and yourself as a leader, you must be equally as boss-like online as you are offline.

Choose your primary platform

When it comes to your personal brand, I would recommend the following channels: LinkedIn, Instagram or Twitter. Each of these platforms can elevate your brand and share your business story depending on your service or product. I will focus on building your personal brand using LinkedIn, but you can use the following guidance for any social media tool.

Identify the goal of your personal brand

Before jumping into building and becoming a boss, let's remember why you should do this exercise. Your personal brand should be used initially for one of four goals – to:

1 Generate income – generate more clients, gain new connections or find opportunities.
2 Find friends and community – build relationships or grow your network.
3 Educate or learn – learn new skills, gain new perspectives or educate yourself.
4 Be seen as an expert or thought leader – share knowledge and educate others.

My advice is to stick to one or two goals when building your boss status online.

How to succeed with LinkedIn

I am not a brand ambassador or influencer for LinkedIn (though if their team is reading this, feel free to drop me a line), but I have seen my life change through the use and misuse of this platform.

I started my LinkedIn journey in January 2019 with no understanding of the platform. Through learning how to best optimize LinkedIn, I have been invited to deliver two TEDx talks, generated 85 per cent of my business opportunities globally, been scouted by leading brands such as Monki to support their gender equality campaigns, and have been referenced as a rising star in social entrepreneurship.

Validate the purpose for building your brand

Your LinkedIn profile should reflect your vision, mission and principle statements. These three concepts will help you build your brand with clarity and relevance.

1   A **vision statement** is where you want to be in the future. It's your big picture and your dream goal.

For example, writing a book on your entrepreneurial journey.

2   A **mission statement** lists the milestones that can help you to achieve that vision. To benefit from your mission, it's effective to coordinate a timeline. Use SMART goals to define your milestones or mini goals.

For example, if writing a book in 18 months, which has 60,000 words, then you must in the first 12 months write 5,000 words each month and, in the last six months, actively look for a publishing house or editor. You want to share updates and references online. This will help to boost your presence in that space.

3   Your **principle statements** are the five topics that you want to be known for, are happy to discuss in conversation or on panels, and align with your overall knowledge areas.

Consider them the five hashtags you could and would use for this goal. Using the same example, you want to be known for your #entrepreneurship #business #leadership #businessjourney #impostersyndrome.

Six ways to optimize your profile

The top half of your LinkedIn profile is the most important. As we discussed in Chapter 4, first impressions count.

- **Clear profile picture** – ensure that your profile picture is clear and relevant to your brand. Unless you are running a selfie business, there's no need for a selfie. Unless you are a founder of an investment bank, you don't need a suit and tie. Your profile picture should be a clear headshot with a clear background, in semi-professional or casual clothing.
- **Customized header** – LinkedIn has a default plain blue header background that appears when you create a profile. Use this space to customize and show your personality or key strengths. Use Paint or Canva to create the header, which can be a picture of London if that's where your business is based, for example. I've used Canva to create a bespoke header for my profile; feel free to visit my profile to get some inspiration.
- **120 characters in your headline** – the section right under your profile picture is your headline and this is where you want to tell your audience about yourself. Consider using the title 'founder' or 'entrepreneur'. If you are a side hustler building your business, then start with your paid corporate title and add your business passion also. You have 120 characters to use, so using vertical bars is a great way to display all this information. For example, my LinkedIn profile says:

Award-Winning Founder @LMFNetwork | Diversity (DE&I) Coach | 2x TEDx Speaker | Top 50 BAME Entrepreneurs & Marie Claire Future Shaper 2020 | ■ Pre-order: Unprepared to Entrepreneur | @sonyabarlowuk

- **Powerful 'about me' section** – on LinkedIn, only the first three lines of your 'about me' section are actually seen by people, as opposed to the whole paragraph, which requires a 'show more' button to be pressed, so make them count. I advise writing in the third person so one can associate your name with your accolades.
- **Filled in experience** – ensure all your experience is listed, with at least three bullet points' worth of detail relevant to your business, brand and future vision.

Five ways to build brand engagement

Engagement on LinkedIn comes over time. The same way you spend 12 weeks in the gym before seeing results, you must be consistent with LinkedIn to see the results. To build long-term value, be seen as a thought leader and draw interest to your business, you must be consistent and relevant:

1 Post or share content at least twice a week.
2 Keep all content relevant and aligned to your five principles; consider them 'hashtags' or reference points.
3 Share and like other people's posts. The algorithm works in your favour if you are engaging with other posts.
4 Use your analytics and data to understand which content works, which products or services raise interest, where your followers are coming from and how you're being searched for.
5 Join the founders' community we have on Slack and share your content, so other founders and community members can like, comment and share.

Similar to the content calendar created for your business brand in Chapter 4, I have created a content calendar for your personal brand, which can be seen in Figure 7.1. Simple yet effective steps such as liking content, sharing content and talking about yourself can help to boost your personal brand. I would recommend you use this as a starting point for six weeks and then create your own once you have explored your personal style.

FIGURE 7.1   Six weeks to success with LinkedIn

	WEEK 1	WEEK 2	WEEK 3	WEEK 4	WEEK 5	WEEK 6
Above		Introduce yourself Like content		Share content Talk about your week		Connect with two new people Share content ×2 Like content ×2 Check your analytics
Below	Update your profile		Like content Share content		Share content ×2 Talk about your week Like content ×2	

The life of a founder is sometimes stressful and can be lonely. If you are confident in yourself, your ability and strengths, you will be able to emerge from any situation with your head high and ready to solve the problem. More often than not, as entrepreneurs we focus more on the business than ourselves. But the truth is that people buy into people and their story. The more of yourself you can show online, the greater your attractiveness will be. Becoming a boss is also about understanding and creating your brand, your style and your personality. It's important that once you have built your profile offline, you can translate this online. The world is your oyster – why would you not want to build a powerful profile to show your purpose?

CASE STUDY   Nadia Edwards-Dashti

Nadia Edwards-Dashti is an award-winning entrepreneur. She is the co-founder of London-based recruitment company Harrington Starr, named as one of *Brummell*'s 2019 Top 30 Inspirational Women in the City and creator of the podcast series called *The DEI Discussions*. Nadia's work is centred around creating inclusive and equitable leadership practices to ensure people can thrive within their roles. As one of the first women in the city to have founded a recruitment business, Nadia understands the problems faced by ordinary people shifting into entrepreneurship. I had the pleasure of interviewing Nadia over Zoom while she balanced running a business and taking care of her one-year-old child while pregnant with her second.

I haven't personally seen many women leading recruitment companies, what encouraged you to step into this industry?

After I graduated university, I started working in the recruitment industry. However, in the early stages, the industry was very male-dominated and leadership styles were authoritarian. Though in practice this meant that there was a structure, it wasn't collaborative or comforting. As a woman entering and progressing in the workplace, I saw leaders around me handle the situations with masculine energy, which wasn't supportive. I am a strong character but not everyone is, and so I wanted to change this and build collaborative recruitment relationships with candidates over time, rather than one-off conversations, which may or may not convert into income.

How did you start Harrington Starr and build/learn how to lead?

Harrington Starr was founded through many random conversations I had with my now co-founders. We all felt a similar sense of frustration and knew that we could do something different – but weren't sure how to take the leap. It wasn't until Toby (my CEO) said 'let's do it' that I handed in my notice and decided to build the company with him. We had a rough idea about what we wanted to build and why. We had no solid training in business or leadership, but had been around enough bad leaders to know what we didn't want to do.

Did you ever feel like an imposter?

Yes. Especially at the start of the journey. I had moments where I felt I wasn't good enough or others wouldn't take me seriously. The way I grew out of that feeling was to always go back to my why – why am I doing this, why did I take a chance on myself? I also leaned into the community around me, shared my pain points and asked for guidance. It was this vulnerability that helped me to grow my client list and leadership skills, and combat imposter syndrome. Now I think, what's the worst that can happen? And give things a go!

You have a number of accolades under your belt, how did you go about achieving these?

As an entrepreneur, you have to be your own biggest cheerleader. What this means is that you must put yourself forward for awards, show evidence of your success and build your brand with clarity, so other people don't question your experience. I use LinkedIn as my main brand profile, sharing my work, the work of my company and many interviews I have conducted through the podcast. As a working mother and entrepreneur, building a brand is time-consuming, and so I tend to focus on using one tool properly rather than spreading myself too thin over a number of platforms.

How can new entrepreneurs empower themselves as great leaders?

I think leaders are not born but made. Anyone can be a leader, as long as they're honest and work hard to evolve. I run a course called *Empowered* which I created for leaders, especially women, who feel they aren't enough. 'Empowered' is an acronym and each letter stands for a task that can be done to find and narrate your leadership style. For example, E is to engage with yourself, others and your colleagues, whereas P is for passion, to showcase this in everything you do and D is to demonstrate your style and brand. In all of this, the running theme is to not be afraid to get it wrong – no one prepares you to lead or start a business – so take comments on board, ask for feedback and educate yourself on good leadership regularly.

Afterthoughts

Becoming a leader starts with believing in yourself as a leader. Entrepreneurs automatically become leaders as they grow their business and their team – however, the rulebook on this doesn't exist. From the examples of Jess and Nadia, we can conclude that one way of finding your leadership style is to exclude the styles of those you didn't consider to be good leaders. Nadia reminds us that entrepreneurs are unprepared, and that's okay and even expected. Her advice reminds us to reflect within, focus on our strengths and involve others in decision making – this builds trust and credibility. In my opinion, leadership is an evolving concept in business and as an entrepreneur, so I wouldn't worry too much if you don't have a solid type of leadership, as long as your intent is aligned to the business goal and growth metrics. Once you find your inner motivation, it's time to share your experience with others and build your brand. Remember, you are the face of your business, so your personality, story and purpose are fundamental in attracting new clients, building relationships and driving revenue into your business.

WORKBOOK

_____

_____

_____

_____

_____

_____

_____

_____

_____

_____

_____

_____

_____

_____

_____

_____

_____

_____

_____

_____

_____

CHAPTER EIGHT

Mind over matter

Let's play a game. The rules are simple: go through the list below and answer each question out loud. Every time you say 'yes', take a sip of water.

Have you ever:

1 Woken up and not wanted to move?
2 Finished a long week and slept for 12 hours straight?
3 Lost yourself on a walk, in a podcast, or while listening to an audiobook?
4 Felt like you will fall at any moment and not be able to get up?
5 Been surrounded by loved ones but still felt alone?

There is no prize for winning this game. All five items are examples of real scenarios that many of us have found ourselves in. These real situations impact our ability to achieve our goals and keep going. These experiences will come up in corporate life as well as the life of an entrepreneur. It's up to us to realize when they may occur, and get help.

One of the reasons I became an entrepreneur is because the corporate world was making me unwell. In 2019, I worked in a day job that didn't align with my strengths and goals. By the end of that year, I found myself on sick leave for five weeks, with a two-week migraine that turned into a cluster headache and a new-found stammer. My emotional and spiritual mental health was at its lowest. I was lost. I decided to focus on being my own boss as it allowed me to control my calendar, adapt working practices to suit my needs and wake up every day wanting to do something I believed in.

And yet, entrepreneurship comes with its own mental health challenges. More often than not when I was searching for inspirational founder stories online, every journey looked perfect and glamorous. Once I started speaking to other entrepreneurs, I learnt that what they didn't share on mainstream media were discussions around working on your business while employed within another. From these conversations, I gauged that in most cases, the average founder works on their side hustle or side business for at least 18 months before going mainstream. I found many had similar stories of investing their own savings into their business (otherwise known as bootstrapping) while carrying out a nine-to-five day job, or burning out from overwork and having to keep going to maintain appearances. It's an area of entrepreneurship no one prepares us for, and can mean the difference between a healthy, sustainable business and one that collapses after an entrepreneur burns out.

Taking care of yourself, learning where to place your energy and ensuring that you are the best version of yourself are important aspects of entrepreneurship. Throughout the chapter, we will hear from several leaders on how they manage their mental health and overall wellness.

What is mental health?

Mental health is a combination of our emotional, psychological and social well-being. It affects how we think, feel and act. Our relationship with our health determines how we handle ourselves and how we manage stress. If we suffer from a mental health condition it can be due to several factors, including biological factors and/or family experiences.

Research conducted by the Mind charity (2020) found that one in four people experience mental health conditions in the UK, and one in six suffer from a common mental health condition in any given week. These statistics are shocking, considering mental well-being is rarely at the top of the agenda in universities and workplaces.

Poor mental health can manifest in different ways, such as feeling burnout, fatigue, guilt, and physical and mental exhaustion. I have experienced this twice. The first time it seemed like a badge of honour to prove that I was working super hard. The second time, I realized how stupid I sounded the first time and promised never to allow myself to reach that state again. Burnout is still a sensitive topic as many employees, employers and entrepreneurs do not like to admit they have experienced it. Either way, burnout is what many of us have experienced but don't realize until it's too late. It's important to have this conversation early so we don't get to that stage.

What are some early warning signs?

In most cases, symptoms rarely flare up overnight. There will be signs to look out for, which can include:

- Mood changes – dramatic shifts in emotions.
- Sleep or appetite changes – decline in personal care and nutrition.
- Withdrawal – loss of interest in activities you previously enjoyed.
- Difficulty thinking – lack of concentration, memory loss or lack of energy that is hard to explain.
- Feeling disconnected – a vague feeling or sense of being removed from reality.

- Apathy – a loss of desire to participate in activities.
- Loss of energy – significant tiredness, low energy or similar feelings.

Though this is not an exhaustive list of the various signs, these are a good starting point. When I was going through my period of stress, I could feel my body asking me to stop and my mind suggesting a break, but the stubbornness in me didn't allow me to pause. During this period of uncertainty, we designed and delivered our first virtual reality event in London. It took me hours to find the energy to go. I coordinated my outfit, wore bright, heeled shoes and applied my favourite shade of lipstick to pick me up. I looked great, but on the inside I was stressed out, worried and on the verge of a breakdown. As the founder, face of the business and solo entrepreneur, it wasn't as easy as asking someone to go in my place. We had spent two months planning, coordinating and prepping. The reality is that sometimes we show up because we have to – not because we want to. And in those moments, we are reminded of how 'well' we look on the outside, which isn't reflective of the inside.

Mental health is a struggle common to many entrepreneurs. Dan Murray-Serter, the co-founder of Heights and the *Secret Leaders* podcast, tells me about the battle that he had with his mental health as an entrepreneur. Dan emphasizes that mental health issues can also be solved with a number of remedies, explaining that 'after several burnout episodes and anxiety', he needed to 'take a step back to look after his health'. He was 'going through depression, anxiety and insomnia'. Despite the doctor's orders to take antidepressants, Dan looked at scientific research and found that adding extra nutrients into his diet might be a good start. He shares that 'DHA omega-3, blueberry extract and B vitamin complex' were the first to have an impact on his health – he went from being unable to sleep to a rested self within ten days, and was sleeping until 7 am. Dan recommends that 'entrepreneurs should remember your brain is your business, and as such it requires fuel to keep running. This fuel consists of a healthy lifestyle, nutrients, rest and days off.' He emphasizes the importance of resting, and that 'fundamentally if you are your business, you aren't a machine'.

Why is this conversation important?

Conversations around mental health are important because it's easy to struggle alone, assume that others are doing fine and believe that you're the only entrepreneur struggling. It's often easy to see news of venture capital funding and acquisitions, and assume that others have an easy path to success. However, entrepreneurs are on a difficult journey with no guaranteed successes. Many work around the clock and face several challenges along the way – staff turnover, rejections from investors and mentors, or just plain old work stress.

A 2013 article in *Inc.* magazine written by Jessica Bruder suggests that 'Entrepreneurs have struggled silently. There's a sense that they can't talk about it, that it's a weakness', while in *Forbes* magazine (Bannon, 2020) it's shared that 'Entrepreneurs are technically 50 per cent more likely to have a mental health condition than ordinary folk, and twice as likely to suffer from depression'. The last quote took me aback. It's great to see that in seven years the narrative around entrepreneurship and mental health is shifting, yet so few people talk about it, and there continues to be limited guidance around it.

At the start of 2020, given the consequences of the Covid-19 pandemic, I realized that more people were interested in starting their own business. One reason might have been because people wanted to take control and have financial independence. Another might have been increased distrust in the system as everything was closed and not everyone was being helped. To support the people who wanted to begin an entrepreneurial journey, in May 2020 I started a podcast called *Strategically Winging It*, where I interviewed and revealed the real stories of great leaders – the good, the bad and the ugly. I also hoped to show that everyone, including me, is strategically winging it.

In one episode, Marine Tanguy, the founder of MTArt agency, shared that she entered the world of entrepreneurship in her early 20s. An advocate for artists since a young age, Marine managed her first gallery at age 21 and opened her first art gallery in Los Angeles at age 23. After seeing the restrictiveness of the traditional gallery model, Marine launched MTArt Agency in 2015. MTArt is the first talent agency for visual artists worldwide. She tells me that she spent years building her resources and network, and overcoming challenges before her business took off. Despite her success, the early years of MTArt Agency were challenging and she found it very hard mentally, as the traditional art sector was so resistant to change. During our conversation, she shared that she suffered bullying and unfair competition on a daily basis. Marine had to learn to look after her mental health during this time and her tips included surrounding yourself with visuals that inspire you, spending time with family and not taking social media too seriously.

In a similar vein, Angelica Malin, the founder of *About Time* magazine, opened up about her journey into entrepreneurship, explaining that at times it was lonely and uncomfortable. Her large social media following and public profile opened her up to being at the centre of many conversations, which can be mentally and emotionally straining. Having spoken about this on the podcast, she shared that to keep herself grounded, she practised self-care routines, took time out of her busy schedule to enjoy moments with loved ones and tried not to worry about making mistakes.

I would encourage anyone who is suffering to reach out to an expert, who will be able to understand their symptoms and help them get better. If you are unsure where to start, please contact me and I will help to answer any queries or connect you with the right people. My email is hello@sonyabarlow.co.uk.

Working cultures

As a founder, your work culture plays a big role in your success and health. On a smaller level, it's your desk space, chair and personal timetable. But it is also the culture you have created for yourself and your team. I know many people who would show up to their office job early in the morning for a breakfast meeting and not leave until late evening. We are talking 12 hours in the same office, for the same company where you're only contracted for seven to nine hours a day. I have also worked for companies that have fake flexible working cultures, meaning they cite 'flexible working' on the job description, but in reality it is frowned upon to choose to work from home or take your full hour's lunch break. It was through these examples that I decided early on that the working culture I wanted to create would be accessible, inclusive and healthy.

The working culture I have implemented for myself includes closing down all technology and stopping all work-related conversation for at least one main meal, taking at least half a day off in the week and reducing my phone time to 30 minutes per call. To be honest, I also limit the workload during my monthly cycle, because in combination with my chronic migraines, it can be intolerable and makes it difficult to concentrate. I take the same energy into my own business; I actively encourage flexible working, for example picking the days of the week one can work (as long as the tasks are completed to deadlines) and advocate taking a day off monthly, as a mental health or recovery day.

In a full-time corporate job, there were days where I would spend up to four hours a day travelling from meeting to meeting. Most of these meetings could have been conducted via a phone call or online meeting rooms. When I questioned the logic of these practices, it was justified as 'the way we've always done things'. As Einstein is famously quoted as saying, 'insanity is doing the same thing over and over and expecting a different result'. Having a toxic working culture, focusing on the timesheets rather than output and then expecting an environment of health and happiness, is contradictory and unreasonable.

As a founder, you must consider the working culture you want to implement. The benefits it has for the business, the team's mental health and overall productivity are immeasurable. This culture is something you must live by yourself, to prove that it's possible before rolling out to the team. You are the business – you need to be your best self for the business to become its best.

Having a healthy relationship with social media

Have you ever gone online for a minute and stayed for an hour?

The Netflix documentary-drama *The Social Dilemma* (2020) educated consumers on the ways social platforms work. They shared that each platform has a group of psychologists whose main goal is to get you back online. The cheek! Hiring people to purposely bring us back online, encouraging us to scroll for hours only to go to bed disheartened by what we have seen. For any social media user, this makes so much sense. The notifications that pop up when you're on a Facebook, Twitter or Instagram feed, the items of clothing you saw in another tab suddenly appearing as promotions and hashtags, which you then follow, sharing content that makes you want to read more. It's addictive and is a marketer's and salesperson's dream.

I used to work at an insights agency, creating and selling media adverts to retailers who encouraged consumers to buy their products by buying media spaces in magazines, promoting their goods through social media, and commissioning influencers to share their experiences. So, I know from first-hand experience the effort and precision that can go into understanding your customer and their habits, and sharing relevant content to lure them back in. Despite knowing the tricks of the trade, whenever I used to go back online, I would become immersed in the feed. One day over the Christmas break, I decided to delete all my social channels and found pure bliss. Turns out, the world didn't end.

Social media has this way of presenting successes in a short caption or an image. When you are already having a bad day, scrolling through this content isn't amusing or encouraging. I remember sitting there comparing myself to others on the platform – acquaintances, friends and community members. I'd question why one person gained more likes on a post than me, why a brand sponsored someone else rather than reaching out to me, and what made one business more attractive than another. I often have phases with social media, deleting the apps when they consume my life or distract me from enjoying the moment. However, I would be lying if I said I was always like this or understood the impact straight away. It was only when my friends and family used to get annoyed with my constant scrolling over our lunch dates that I knew I had to stop.

Hersha Patel, a TV presenter, actress, entrepreneur and comedian sat down with me over a coffee in London to discuss her relationship with mental health. She shares that she found her way back to health by nourishing her mind and body through veganism, workouts and focusing on her spiritual well-being, and began to rely less on her career and social media to determine her self-worth. The moment she stepped away from being online she unwittingly became the victim of a global shaming when Nigel Ng, a comedian and YouTuber, poked fun at a video she was featured in. The video swept the globe and quickly clocked up millions of views; she was mercilessly trolled and felt under attack. Instead of shutting down her account 'which was my first instinct', she took it upon herself to try to change the narrative, with great success 'I genuinely believe that I managed to turn it from a negative to a positive because of all the spiritual work I have done on myself. I had the tools to deal with the intense stress and anxiety that was a very real online character assassination and bullying that could have destroyed my mental health.' To cater to her mental health and well-being, Hersha recommends 'rely on sticking to a digital routine, creating content over many days before posting it online and not worrying about immediate success, because the definition of success will differ for everyone and you may go viral overnight without even knowing.' She also shared that taking care of your mind, soul and body, even if that means taking time off and away from everything, is the best thing an individual can do for themselves and the future of their business.

Here are four things I can share, which have helped me:

1 **Manage your calendar** – allot different days for different focus areas. For example, Monday can be administrative, Tuesday for team meetings and Friday can be for finance. In addition to this, colour code your calendar meetings to identify which are of high priority, ie urgent, and low priority, ie your business won't crumble if these aren't met. And lastly, book out one hour for lunch and 15 minutes walking time daily, so that you can take a break.

2 **Prioritize your business-critical tasks** – list all your tasks at the start of the day and prioritize into high, low and medium. Don't check your notifications and social media platforms until you have completed the high- and medium-priority tasks.

3 **Schedule content** – this can be scheduling emails the evening before to go out the next day or planning social media content as we discussed in Chapter 4. I found myself forgetting to reply to emails, so every other Sunday I would spend one hour going through the week's meetings, writing replies and scheduling emails to go out first thing Monday morning.

4 **Don't compare** – you must remind yourself that the online world is not reality, but a snapshot of someone's life. Don't fall into the trap of comparing yourself to others, because the

truth is that just as others don't know the many hurdles you are jumping daily, you don't know theirs either. I often find myself scrolling through media for hours comparing and contrasting. Once I consciously see myself doing this, I turn my phone off and focus on my business.

No one will be looking over your shoulder asking if you are doing the work and checking if you are okay. As a leader, you must identify when something isn't okay, what isn't working and find real solutions.

Dealing with loneliness

Among the myriad mental health and wellness-related issues that entrepreneurs face, loneliness is one that I found myself dealing with. According to the CEO Snapshot Survey, led by Thomas J Saporito in 2012, nearly 70 per cent of first-time CEOs suffer from loneliness and 61 per cent believe that it hinders their performance (Saporito, 2012). Though the data itself is a few years old, the sentiment feels relevant. It's difficult being alone, whether you're at the top of the organization or a first-time entrepreneur. This is an area of entrepreneurship no one prepares you for. It can feel like no one understands you, no one is there to listen to your ideas and you are overwhelmed with tasks to complete before the day ends. Your negative thoughts start small, like seeds, and grow into large plants inside of your mind.

Loneliness comes from a lack of belonging, a term coined by psychologist Abraham Maslow. Maslow's hierarchy of needs (1954) was one of the first theories that shared that before a person grows in self-esteem or confidence, they need to feel love and a sense of belonging (McLeod, 2006). The longer a person goes without this satisfaction, the more they long for it. Belonging is the third level of the hierarchy, cited after basic psychological and safety needs. In this instance, it's defined as interpersonal relationships and feeling like you're a part of a group.

In 2019, I proposed that Maslow's hierarchy itself needs to be adapted, considering the changes the digital age and the internet have brought with them. Once basic psychological needs are met, technology is an enabler to help one find community and eventually confidence. I explained this model in Figure 8.1.

In 2019, in my first TEDx Talk 'Please come online', I shared that being lonely was one of the reasons I founded the LMF Network. For me, loneliness was associated with a lack of purpose and the absence of friendships. It's widely quoted that 90 per cent of the global population is looking for connectivity (Gevelber, 2013) and I believe that technology can support us by helping us access new networks. At the same time, we must reflect on how we feel and why we want relationships with others. Loneliness isn't always about people, but about our relationship with ourselves when we are alone. I had times I couldn't stand being alone, but once I found my purpose this was slowly no longer the case.

FIGURE 8.1   Barlow hierarchy of needs

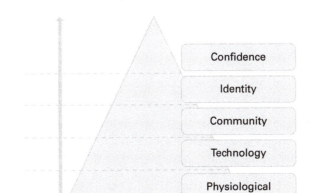

Once I was able to overcome the initial hurdle of feeling ashamed when I asked for help, I found myself no longer feeling lonely or like I didn't belong. I have accepted that I can ask for help and lean on others in troubling times. Many entrepreneurs go through the same process, and so have many anecdotes to share. Entrepreneurship can allow you to lean on your community in a way that many other roles do not.

Some things you can do today to lessen feeling lonely include:

• connecting with other entrepreneurs online;
• scheduling co-working sessions or virtual coffee meets;
• meditating to control your negative thoughts;
• allowing yourself to cry or feel the emotions;
• talking it out.

As with anything, time is a great healer. So have faith in yourself and the journey you are on.

How to deal with your mental health as an entrepreneur

Mental health concerns are real and it's time we gave them the focus they deserve. This chapter is about changing the narrative around open mental health discussions so that you and your team can grow.

Here are ten ways you can deal with mental (and general) health scenarios:

1 **Recognize the signs and symptoms.** The first step to finding your solution is to identify your signs and symptoms. Make a list of what you think you feel, journal examples or times where such emotions are heightened and track your progress.
2 **Network to find your community.** Use the networking tools and the concept of communities shared in Chapter 5 for your business and yourself. Find your people through searching

for 'entrepreneur meetups', sharing a post on LinkedIn or joining our Slack channel.

3 **Change your working culture.** As discussed above, your style and place of work can cause mental health conditions you didn't consider. Take a moment to audit your work culture – is it healthy, productive and prosperous? If not, you know what to do.

4 **Find a mentoring group.** One area of development that is underrated is mentoring. Mentoring is the relationship between two or more people who share knowledge, understanding and supporting one another through defined objectives. The groups are a great way to share problems confidentially and safely, where every member wants to contribute to solving them.

5 **Make time for yourself and loved ones.** Your sanity, self-care and time with your loved ones can be considered the 'mental health foundation' of your business. As an entrepreneur, you can get lost in your world. Dedicate time to yourself, indulge in non-work-related activities and enjoy time with loved ones in a setting outside the workspace.

6 **Exercise or invest in a healthier routine.** They say 'you are what you eat', so by investing in a healthy meal plan that includes fruit and vegetables, and taking time for exercise or meditation, you are building all the muscles within your body and nurturing them to keep you going for longer. For example, research shows that blueberries are great for keeping your blood pressure low, and can help maintain brain functions (Harvard Health, 2019). A top tip is every time your brain wanders, go for a little walk, even if it's around your living space, to get the blood flowing.

7 **Limit your digital devices and time spent online.** The internet is a portal of information, and misinformation. Limit your screen time by scheduling time when you are available, use free plugins such as Calendly to manage your calendar and delete social apps from your phone when required. As

someone who has tried and tested these things, I can tell you that this was one of the changes that provided the greatest support for me.

8 **Reflect on your goals and successes.** Sometimes, I think our mental health conditions grow because we have lost focus on what's important, what we are aiming for and how far we have come. Take a moment to reflect on your goals, document what you have achieved so far and praise yourself for your accomplishments.

9 **Get help.** There is a taboo around therapy, especially in the South Asian and Black communities. Therapy isn't a sign of weakness. If you can, get help through a therapist, counsellor or free helpline and take yourself out of that problem state.

10 **Take a break.** Sometimes, you just have to take a break. Stop, book a holiday, take some leave and enjoy the flexibility of becoming an entrepreneur.

Mental health issues are nothing to be afraid of. Sometimes, it's a good reminder that you have a heart and are human. The more of us who start this conversation, the easier it will be. You may feel like giving up and like you need a rest – take that time off, relax, and return refreshed. Once you overcome your hurdles, the rest becomes easier.

CASE STUDY   Hussain Manawer

Hussain Manawer is a British poet, performer and producer. He is a renowned mental health activist who has won critical acclaim for his ability to drag stigma kicking and screaming into the light with his timeless talent. Since his initial entry into entrepreneurship, Hussain has lost his mother, which has led him to pivot his career from entertainment to education. Hussain's work raises awareness of mental health and community. He is currently an Honorary Fellow of the prestigious King's College London, has received an Honorary Doctorate from Oxford Brookes University and in 2017 set the Guinness World Record for the world's largest mental health awareness lesson.

Hussain's House launched in 2013. What was the purpose behind this business?

Hussain's House was my way of bringing everyone together and opening up the spaces around topics that we didn't traditionally discuss. Growing up in Ilford, I hadn't thought that I could meet or talk to televised celebrities such as Kevin Hart, but I wanted to try. Not for anything other than to have a conversation with him about his career, entertainment and being a person of colour creative. The initial platform was YouTube, because it allowed me to upload video content and it was free.

How did you get your conversations or clients?

In all honesty, I made a list of people I wanted to interview, found their agents and sent them emails. This approach seems old school but cold calling and cold emails worked for me. I didn't initially think such big names would respond, but at the same time I had nothing to lose. It was all about giving yourself and your vision a go!

Since Hussain's House, you have moved into the poetry and mental health space, please can you explain how made that pivot?

Mental health was something I have always been serious about, especially as it's a topic that isn't centre stage in Asian households. Unfortunately, my mother passed away a few years ago and it shocked my system. I felt lost and alone. The material things didn't matter because I realized how precious life and family were. Long story short, I became depressed and unwell. Through this experience, rather than shy away, I started to document my journey to get better through platforms such as Instagram and Twitter. Through this content, I was able to generate new awareness and expose these topics in mainstream media, which is now the foundation of my work.

What have you learnt since starting on your journey to bring mindfulness over matter?

I have consciously taken steps to keep myself healthy. This includes focusing on my diet, eating the right nutrients, exercising and taking myself off social media. As a business and brand, it can be easy to lose yourself in the clout of social media and feeling like you always have to be online. In reality, no one is going to miss you if you don't post online, and your business won't be the best it can be if you aren't feeling your best.

What is your advice for entrepreneurs who find themselves balancing being online and staying sane?

Focus on your why – why does your business exist, why does your brand matter, why are you doing what you're doing? Any time you have a negative or bad moment, go back to your why and remind yourself of your purpose. From experience of growing a large following and social presence, what people say or think about you isn't your business – leading your business into success is. All in all, as an entrepreneur your mental health matters more than anything, because without your mental sanity and muscle, you are left with nothing. And that nothing itself, is very lonely.

Afterthoughts

Mental health and entrepreneurship go hand in hand. Working at full capacity and not recharging your batteries is not going to be good for your body or business. Hussain outlines that we should prioritize ourselves and always go back to our 'why'. Similarly, Hersha mentions that after her burnout, it was her 'why' that got her going and healthy. In my experience as a founder, mental health is not discussed enough and yet we as business owners can control our calendars – this is powerful. If we have the ability to prioritize, it's time to focus on our mind working for us 100 per cent rather than chasing the things that don't matter.

EXERCISE

This exercise will help you prioritize your workload and your health.

• Colour code your calendar, with different colours identifying priority meetings and tasks, and move those items that don't align with your business priorities.

• Add an automated out-of-office message to your email, linking to any useful resources and setting expectations (or boundaries) for when someone can expect a reply.

• Schedule 15 minutes daily in your calendar for a walk, away from all technology and media.

WORKBOOK

CHAPTER NINE

Shifting your money mindset

Operating your own business is a dream come true, but it will fail if your finances aren't in order. It is important to manage your finances and ensure that you can generate revenue sustainably to meet your business's long-term goals. What we don't want is for your first year to be a success and then for your bottom line to go into a loss in subsequent years.

I remember opening my laptop, going onto Google, and typing in 'how to make money as an entrepreneur'. To my surprise, much of the information was strategies, not financial education 101. The content felt scattered and unclear, with no clear direction or starting point. I hadn't a clue which comes first – the cash flow, budget, or profit and loss statement.

I had many questions:

How do I budget for my expenses and do I have to charge VAT?

What is the difference between venture capital and grant-based funding, and when should I take it?

How do I manage the inflow and outflow of cash?

What sources of finance are available?

What I soon learned was that to grow your business you must learn to take care of finances from the start – align strategies to meet monetary goals, simplify business processes and ensure that budgets are kept to a minimum.

This chapter is finance 101 for entrepreneurs. We will discuss what money really means, how to generate growth through various income streams, how to diversify your portfolio and how to receive backing from a venture fund.

Why do we need to discuss finances?

One of the main objectives of running a business is to generate revenue in order to stay afloat. By having an honest conversation about finances, you will be able to:

- anticipate the future financial needs of the business;
- assess risks to which the business may be exposed;
- help the decision-making process, and investors and lenders to evaluate their investments and loans based on both qualitative and quantitative measures;
- distinguish between personal and business finances;
- better understand financial products as a consumer and entrepreneur;
- ensure your finances comply with country-specific regulations;
- exercise financial control and management;
- improve efficiencies within the business;
- demonstrate your ability as a steward (meaning that you manage the business's finances on behalf of shareholders).

I feared financial discussions because I often believed they would remind me that I wasn't doing enough. Once I confronted this fear, my idea went from a passion project to a viable business.

Spend time understanding your costs

A key mistake I made in the beginning, as an entrepreneur, was registering my business without understanding the costs associated, such as accounting fees. I could have done a more thorough review of the different forms of doing business, eg being a sole trader of self-employed. Instead, I chose to register as a limited company, as that is the most common form of doing business in the UK. Another area I struggled with was investing money back into the business. I made it an aim to hold on to cash, due to fear of misspending or seeing hard-earned revenue decrease; I managed the accounts myself and never sought out professional help.

I set up the LMF Network as a limited company through Companies House, the UK-based agency that incorporates and dissolves companies. The costs of setting up my company in the UK in 2019 and having to pay professional services fees meant that in my first year of business I only made a small profit. However, that profit wasn't mine to take as I had to reinvest it into the company's website and domain, give our volunteers thank you gifts and pay for expenses. In 2020, I decided to convert into a community interest company (CIC), which meant closing the limited company and building a new financial model to generate revenue. Little did I know that the Covid-19 pandemic would strike, leaving us in the red, spending money we didn't have as revenue streams started drying up and sponsors stepped back because of budget cuts and financial constraints. This meant I had to use my personal savings to cover software costs such as Zoom, Gmail and LinkedIn Live. This setback eroded all projections for 2020.

By the end of year two, I was unsure of what to do next. My business had just about broken even, which at the time felt like a failure. I immersed myself in financial education, asking for help and seeking advice from other entrepreneurs.

Businesses set out to be profitable so they can cover their basic costs. However, we must know what these costs are. Your business won't grow unless your revenue-generating model is sustainable.

Shifting your money mindset

In a corporate job, you have stability from your salary. As an entrepreneur, your revenue and salary can vary greatly from month to month.

LMF Network has been rejected twice for grant funding and sponsorships, two avenues we thought would provide financial stability and security. The old Sonya may have given up; the new me took this as a sign to change direction and model.

A part of me felt like an imposter because I wasn't able to sustain the original business model. I decided it was time to start my own consultancy as my money-generating stream.

LMF Network's mission was to stay true to social good, with 50 per cent of all net cash reinvested into the organization. In order to do so, I had to redo my 2020 cash flow forecast and create a more realistic one for 2021.

The cash flow forecast is a document that shows how money moves in and out of your business. The cash flow can be fairly simple, as shown in the example in Table 9.1, identifying the main inflows as grants, operations and sponsorship; and outflows as staff or operation costs.

As you can see in the example in Table 9.2, in 2021 we would generate £18,000 worth of grants and £8,000 worth of sponsorship. Despite operational costs, we would be able to compensate interns or volunteers for their time and end the year in the black with £13,240. It was also decided that the other LMF branches would be responsible for their own cash flow and accounts, after being provided with a fixed amount per month for franchising costs and a percentage of their income every year.

TABLE 9.1   Example cash flow forecast

		Date			
	1Q20	2Q20	3Q20	4Q20	FY20
Inflow from grants		£7,500	£0	£0	£7,500
Inflow from operations		£5,000	£250	£0	£5,250
Recurring from sponsorship		£750	£750	£750	£2,250
Total inflow	**£0**	**£13,250**	**£1,000**	**£750**	**£15,000**
Recurring staff costs		–£600	–£600	–£600	–£1,800
Other operating costs		£0	£0	£0	£0
Net cash before reinvestment		**£12,650**	**£400**	**£150**	**£13,200**
Reinvestment		–£10,120	–£320	–£120	£11,400
EBITDA (Earnings before interest tax dividends and amortization)		**£2,530**	**£80**	**£30**	**£24,600**

In real terms, once the figures were laid out so neatly on the page, it felt like things were about to get serious. In order to achieve £13,240 as profit, I had to re-evaluate our ways of working and how I managed money.

TABLE 9.2   Example cash flow forecast

	Date				
	1Q21	2Q21	3Q21	4Q21	FY21
Inflow from grants	£2,000	£4,000	£9,000	£3,000	£18,000
Inflow from operations	£800	£800	£1,000	£1,200	£3,800
Recurring from sponsorship	£2,000	£1,000	£3,000	£2,000	£8,000
Inflow from LMF Toronto	£120	£120	£120	£120	£480
Total inflow	**£4,920**	**£5,920**	**£13,120**	**£6,320**	**£30,280**
Recurring staff costs	–£500	–£500	–£1,000	–£1,000	-£3,000
Other operating costs	–£200	–£200	–£200	–£200	–£800
Net cash before reinvestment	**£4,220**	**£5,220**	**£11,920**	**£5,120**	**£26,480**
Reinvestment	–£2,110	–£2,610	–£5,960	–£2,560	–£13,240
EBITDA (Earnings before interest, tax dividends and amortization)	**£2,110**	**£2,610**	**£5,960**	**£2,560**	**£13,240**

Four ways to start shifting your money mindset

1 **Identify** – identify what your financial goals are and why. Once you can identify your goals, you can create plans and practical steps to achieve them. Similar to goal-setting exercises, you should also set time constraints.

2 **Shift** – shift your mindset from scarcity to abundance. I stopped thinking about what I didn't have and focused on what I did have, what was accessible and what could be free. For example, I realized that Canva offered a discount for not-for-profits, as did many businesses once you explained your model to them. Before I made any financial business decisions, I looked into the accounts to ensure we could cover at least three months of fixed overheads. The concept of ensuring that upcoming expenses (liabilities) can be met as they fall is essential for the continued success of a business and also in maintaining your business reputation.

3 **Switch the narrative** – there are various limiting beliefs about money that should be avoided. As a first-time entrepreneur, this includes thoughts like 'it's my first year, I can't earn that much' or 'why would someone want to invest in me?'

4 **Find gratitude** – be grateful for what you have, enjoy the journey you're on and celebrate every win. This is not important just for finances, but in general as an entrepreneur. At every crossroad, we must take a moment to reflect on how far we've come and how we must keep moving forward.

Timi Merriman-Johnson, the founder of Mr MoneyJar, shares that 'starting a business can be one of the most exciting yet riskiest things you can ever do'. When it comes to shifting the money mindset, it is as important to have an eye on the future as it is to have an eye on the day-to-day running of your business. He recommends 'paying into a pension, saving an emergency fund and keeping cash reserves in your business as things you can do while building your business in the here and now'. This ensures that whether you go on to build the next Amazon or not, you have all bases covered.

Studies have shown that up to 82 per cent of businesses fail because of poor cash flow management (Flint, 2020). Keeping a record of how much money you can expect to receive in your business and when will allow you to plan, make decisions and operate with certainty.

What is a budget?

A budget is a plan of how much money to set aside for future expenditure. If the Covid-19 pandemic taught me anything, it was that your income can be stopped overnight – then what?

How to create a budget

You can begin by asking yourself these questions:

- What are the project's sales for the period in question?
- What are the direct costs of sales (eg cost of materials)?
- What are the fixed costs or overheads (eg cost of premises, utilities, vehicle expenses, travel, legal, advertising, etc)?
- What are the costs for employees, including myself? (This one I found difficult to implement because I reinvest what we make. As an entrepreneur your monthly income can differ depending on the costs incurred and if you are offering any group benefits, such as health care, pension contribution or supplying technology tools.)
- What is the anticipated expenditure on tax this year?

Each business model will incur different costs depending on the size and operation model. It's important to educate yourself on your local regulations before setting up your budget, to ensure everything is covered.

What should your budget include?

- **Projected cash flow** – your expected cash position and monthly projections.

- **Costs** – The costs associated with running a business:
  - ○ fixed – items such as rent, salaries, financing costs;
  - ○ variable – items such as raw materials and overtime;
  - ○ one-off – items such as one-off purchasing of a laptop.
- **Revenues** – anticipated income streams that you can expect to generate.
- **Expected vs actual** – columns to clearly define what you projected versus what was actually delivered. This can be used as a guide to not only benchmark how relevant your budgeting was but can also be used as a tool to improve future budgeting. If you find yourself straying too far away from projected figures, it is important to take some time to understand why. If this persists, there is clearly some fundamental issue in your cash flow management that needs to be addressed before moving further.

Table 9.3 is an example of a basic budget sheet. You can find many free downloadable templates online if you aren't sure how to create your own.

Now that I've got my budget, what should I do?

You should review your budgets monthly and share them with your shareholders, advisory board or team on a quarterly basis. Within the LMF Network, each quarter we share our updated budgets, cash flows and projected costs with our team. This allows for better communication, stronger relationships and loyalty. Furthermore, it creates a culture of accountability.

What is the 50:30:20 rule?

The 50:30:20 budget rule originates from the 2006 book *All Your Worth*, written by Elizabeth Warren and Amelia Warren Tyagi. This rule suggests that 50 per cent of your income should go towards essentials, including paying off debts and paying staff, 30 per cent towards the 'wants' and 20 per cent into your emergency fund.

TABLE 9.3 Budget sheet

Select reporting month	Month 01		Date
FULL YEAR	**Budget**	**Actual**	**Difference**
Operating revenue			
Non-operating revenue			
Total revenue			
Total expenses			
Profit			
YEAR TO DATE	**Budget**	**Actual**	**Difference**
Operating revenue			
Non-operating revenue			
Total revenue			
Total expenses			
Profit			
MONTH	**Budget**	**Actual**	**Difference**
Operating revenue			
Non-operating revenue			
Total revenue			
Total expenses			
Profit			

How do I apply the 50:30:20 rule to my business?

1 **Calculate your income after tax** – your after-tax income will be your revenue minus all costs and business expenses. This is where you could amortize costs over the long term to adjust your profits. For example, a computer may cost £1,000. However, this is an asset that will last five years but you have taken the cost in your first year when revenues are low. You could amortize the cost over the five years for £200 a year instead of hitting the P&L for the full £1,000. This all depends on what standard you are using when preparing your financial statements.

2 **Categorize your income for the past month** – to see a true statement of your monthly finances, use your budget planner and bank statements. Split all your expenses into three categories: needs, wants and savings.

3 **Evaluate and adjust** – now you can see where your income is going and you can actively adjust your lifestyle to support the business's needs and growth.

While doing the same activity for myself, I found that colour-coding items kept the lines around income and expenses clear. As an additional method of keeping tabs on your finances, I recommend creating a spreadsheet with new business deals, projected and secured. For these, add additional columns to represent invoices sent and paid.

Managing expenses

Managing expenses is not a difficult task and yet, I always find myself struggling. I'd often forget and end up scrolling through my bank statements at the end of each month, tallying up the expenditure.

Here's a rundown of how to do expenses every month. I'd recommend dedicating half a day each month, to keep yourself on track:

1 **Embrace technology** – take photos of your expenses and upload them into separate Google folders by month, or straight into your accounting software (examples of which include Xero, Quickbooks and Excel). I would personally recommend Google Sheets, as it is free and allows for more than one person to share the sheet if required. This way, your team and accountant can have the same visibility as you do.

2 **Categorize these into the correct functions** – basic functions include business, marketing, legal, transport and subsistence.

3 **Calculate the cash** – note down each monthly expense total in a spreadsheet, which can be shared with your accountant at the end of each tax year.

I have my finances in order, what next?

Once you have your expenses, cash flow and budgets in order, it's time to consider *if* and how you will generate additional revenue. If you decide that extra funding is required, there are several routes you can consider.

Sources of funding

Small business loans are traditional business loans that you can borrow from a financial institution. These loans should be considered debt finance, which you are obligated to pay back with interest.

Startup loans are low-interest loans available from governments. These schemes often come with additional features such as professional support, mentoring or free accounting software.

Business accelerators are programmes that offer developing startups a small investment, mentoring, office space and networks in exchange for equity. These programmes can be over a long time period but can be competitive. Examples include Y Combinator, Techstars and Deutsche Bank's Tech Accelerator Programme.

Business overdrafts are similar to personal overdrafts – when your bank balance goes to zero you can carry on spending until the pre-set limit is reached. Overdrafts are useful if your business operates on a seasonal basis. They can come with high interest rates and banks can demand their money back at any time, with interest. If this is an option you are considering, I would recommend always talking to a trained financial advisor on the viability of this option.

Business credit cards can be a handy source of financing for entrepreneurs. If possible, you should avoid using a credit card to start a business, as you're already entering into a debt period with high interest rates. If this is an option you are considering, I would recommend always talking to a trained financial advisor on the viability of this option.

Qualified accountants Rizwaan Khan and Hetal Pratapshinh share that the most common area entrepreneurs want advice on is money and credit. They advise that business credit cards should not be relied on as a way to fund the business but from an operational point of view, they should certainly be used to pay ongoing expenses, as the assurance and cover provided by your credit card company is much needed for a small firm. Despite the need to finance being fundamental in the running of a business, many entrepreneurs are unaware of how best to manage their finances to ensure long-term growth.

Crowdfunding platforms allow you to raise funds from people, either for equity or reward. Useful crowdfunding platforms include Kickstarter, Crowdcube and GoFundMe.

Alex Stephany, the founder of Beam, shares his experience of crowdfunding to train and support homeless people in the workplace. His idea 'came to him after building a friendship with a homeless man outside his tube station' and realizing that this man 'had a huge potential but lacked support or a way of overcoming the financial barriers that stood in his way'. The idea came in 2016 and after over half a year spent developing the model with people with lived experience of homelessness and London-based charities, Alex launched Beam in 2017 with his business partner, who himself came from a background working in drug and alcohol services and social care. He shares that 'crowdfunding was a new collaborative way to approach homelessness that could remove barriers while giving people new support networks from the people who'd funded their campaigns on beam.org'.

Personal savings can include your personal savings or investment from friends and family. This type of funding allows you to keep 100 per cent equity in your business.

Business angels are private investors, normally former entrepreneurs or wealthy individuals, who invest in startups for an equity stake. When taking on an investor, make sure to do your due diligence to understand their ways of working, whether through their previous companies and exit strategies, or fellow investments. Their stake means that they have control in the business and can be considered an external partner. This style of funding can also come with mentoring, advice and guidance.

Khaleelah Jones, founder of Careful Feet Digital, shares that she 'initially was hesitant about growing her business outside of bootstrapping' as she 'didn't want to lose equity or ownership'. However, once the business started to grow she soon realized that without outside funding it wouldn't have been able to scale. Khaleelah eventually went down the angel investor route with investment from a mentor, who was someone she already knew. Khaleelah shares that she picked an investor she knew (and was picky in the process) because 'the terms and conditions other investors placed on the table weren't acceptable. For example, asking for too much equity in the business, or limiting my salary despite running a profitable business. As a woman of colour, I worked hard to build the business from an idea and felt that such demands diminished my role as a founder.' I have heard in many instances that working with investors is a stronger relationship than marriage and so should be approached with caution.

Venture capitalists (VC) invest large sums of money into expanding businesses, with tremendous growth potential. Companies such as Airbnb, Spotify and Facebook have all grown thanks to VC investment. With VCs, there is no obligation to pay back the money borrowed from them, though many investors will ask for equity shares or a seat at the table. VCs want a clear exit strategy and expect higher returns. It's important to note that VC funds historically have high expectations for growth metrics and one should be cognizant of what they're going into.

Lena Chauhan, founder of Rise IQ and ex-founder of Market Securities, shared that she ultimately 'decided not to use VC funding for her startup'. Lena launched Rise IQ in 2018 to guide employees through their health journey. Soon after, some of her own family members and community were diagnosed with dementia. She built and validated a web app to help people affected by dementia, in partnership with UCL Dementia Research. Like many entrepreneurs, Lena sought alternative funding to help scale her product. Initially considering VC funding, Lena tells me that the 'vision between herself and potential investors was not aligned'. Despite being offered funding, Lena pulled out as she recalls 'the VC model often focuses on the million-dollar moonshot business as the end goal, which doesn't necessarily mean it will support a social purpose. My own goal, after being a carer, was to create a positive social impact. I eventually sold the web app in 2019 to a larger distributor with whom my purpose and vision were aligned.' Lena's example provides clarity to a topic many entrepreneurs may not realize – partnering with a VC fund is a long-term investment and relationship from both sides and should only be done if you are happy with the measure of success.

Small business grants are provided by local authorities and private organizations to support economic development in a certain area. It's worth considering that such grants often have long application processes.

Local councils and banks also often have proposals. At the start of 2020 for example, the UK chancellor announced small business loans with favourable terms to support those who had been impacted by the pandemic. Similarly, the Mayor of London announced startup business grants for small businesses focused on sustainability and community development.

Hera Hussain, the founder of Chayn, a tech collective that supports survivors of gender-based violence globally, says she chose the slow and measured growth route and took funding from grants and charitable donations. 'Once you get a grant from a well-established, old funder – suddenly many other funders see you as credible. We were able to break into this by pairing with another organization that had a long history of receiving successful grants despite being a small team and they became the lead applicant. After that and many failed attempts later, now I know what funders are looking for and have been able to raise almost £500,000 in the space of two years. It's almost unbelievable when I think back to the £5,000–£7,000 we operated on for the first few years of the organization.'

In most cases, charitable donations require an application. Hera explains that funders are looking for an impactful story, clarity of focus and set success measurables. Grants are mostly awarded to those who can prove valuable in their proposed business activity. I echo Hera's viewpoint that once you are able to secure funding, it's much easier to secure more. These grants can be highly competitive. LMF Network was rejected by the National Lottery grant twice in 12 months before finally being awarded a grant for £9,000. The benefit of using a grant is that you have more control over how it's spent and can funnel it into the business over a longer period of time.

In some ways, financing your business has never been easier. If you are unsure about the right step, I would highly recommend reaching out to your network, either directly or by attending relevant events.

Five ways to reinvest financial revenue to grow your business

Though it's important to pay yourself for your hard work as an entrepreneur, I decided to reinvest my own earnings back into the network to support its growth. Here are five areas to consider reinvesting your revenue into:

1 **Business improvement** – most startups spend their initial profits in reinvesting and as an entrepreneur, your startup should be no exception. Your reinvestment plans should be in line with your strategic goals. Most businesses choose to reinvest in infrastructure, equipment, streamlining processes and the improvement of customer service.

2 **The team** – a better and happier workforce will increase productivity and create the kind of culture that attracts hardworking talent. Reinvest your profits in human resources initiatives, such as training, coaching and continuous education. Maintaining a happy employee culture is more cost-effective than hiring new employees, which can cost about three to six months' worth of lost time and salary.

3 **Marketing** – digital marketing is a smart investment to boost your business if it's done right. Focus on your marketing goals, ask for help if required and track social marketing campaigns to ensure impact. This can be a great extra boost to attract new customers to your business.

4 **Outsource your least favourite tasks** – focusing on tasks that do not serve you isn't the best use of your time. Outsourcing tasks and hiring help creates long-term efficiencies and keeps you working on the things that really matter, like new business, leadership and social marketing.

5 **Create a cash buffer** – while reinvesting in your business is great, ensure that you have enough cash for a rainy day to avoid any disasters. It is always advisable to have liquid assets available for when you really need them.

There is no right or wrong way to use your hard-earned revenue. However, the advice here is always to make decisions based on your strategic, long-term business plans rather than in-the-moment excitement.

Many of us don't have the knowledge required to discuss and make adequate decisions on our finances. If I could turn back the clock, the first thing I would do differently is note down all my business income streams and projected income. The second would be to present this information to a fellow entrepreneur to see if it made sense. Then, I'd educate myself on finances from an accounting perspective. This is where your network comes in – don't be afraid to ask questions. Lean on your community, mentors and accountants for advice. Once I was able to get my funds in order, despite feeling scared to open that initial bank statement, the future was brighter. By understanding from where I was starting and failing, I was able to define what success looks like for our business and streamline the business model to ensure long-term sustainable growth.

CASE STUDY   Devina Paul

Devina Paul is the founding partner of Galvanise Capital and a board member of several companies. She is a serial entrepreneur who has launched a number of financial and services businesses. She is the Chief Financial Officer (CFO) for Zumo and advises startups on sustainable growth.

How would you define what you do in finance?

Put simply: I get a business funded and sale-ready.

As a founder, can you tell us about your experience as an entrepreneur?

In 2012, I decided to take the leap from employee to entrepreneur to consult and advise companies on how to best grow their business, stay financially competitive and ensure that they are able to scale. My job was to go in, secure the business financials and meet the exit strategy.

What is your advice for first-time entrepreneurs who are focusing on finances?

I would say it's that you have to make sure you are 'financially literate.' You have to do the work – it translates when you go out to find and ask for funding. You need to understand your cash flow and profit & loss (P&L) statements. You don't need to understand everything, but basic accounting you should know. You want to be able to hand someone the work and have enough knowledge to sense-check it, as ultimately it's your business and your responsibility.

A P&L and cash flow statement are the key statements to manage your business day to day. The balance sheet is the indication of your financial health. All three statements are necessary in understanding how much money you need, why you need it and how you will fund it.

How did you fund your first solo business?

Before I took the leap, I was given a great piece of advice and that was to ensure I have a six-month buffer. What this ultimately meant was that I had saved six months' worth of emergency funding to cover all the necessities to stay afloat. This helped fuel passion to generate more funds but comfort to know that I was able to keep the roof over my head. Six months is enough time to see if you can get some traction and if your model is viable. I was lucky enough to have two clients who carried on and believed in the vision.

How did you grow your business?

Simply put, our network knew what we were doing and wanted a part of the action. This is a great example of taking others on the journey with you. Our mutual networks and communities wanted to invest their money, add value through partnerships and support businesses to grow – because we had already been in a similar space, they believed we were capable and invested their funds into our model.

How did you enter the world of angel investing?

When I was working for a corporate, my now founding partner was my then managing director. We had worked together to grow and sell a business and we're aware of each other's skills. I enjoyed the process of working with a company, supporting it through mentoring and investment and then exiting for a win. My founder had a similar idea to what I did, so when he approached me and our third co-founder to start Galvanise, it was hard to turn down. Angel investing naturally came as a next step, through my passion for investing, supporting and exiting businesses. We identified that people were not offering the full service to early-stage businesses, so that was where our niche transformed into our USP (unique selling point).

How can businesses that go to investors make the most out of the relationship?

Some investors also want to be a value-add, meaning they are open to mentoring, coaching and opening up their black book to support businesses to grow. If you as an entrepreneur are looking for funding and money to keep going, don't be afraid to reach out to your network and ask them for more than just funds; more often than not they are happy to lend a hand in other ways. My advice would be to know what you need and be honest about the support so that the investor can also meet the expectations and be on the same page. Any financial relationship is a serious investment, because fundamentally no matter where you gain the funding from, the other party wants to make sure it's used in the best way possible.

What do entrepreneurs often forget about when approaching business angels?

The investment process is often the hardest part because many companies aren't set up in the way they should be. The process always takes longer than you think it may. Early-stage businesses that are considering an investment need to make sure they are coordinating due diligence, contracts and business cases from the start, and have them to hand. The foundations you have to have in your business to make the investment process easier: the cash flow, business plan, equity ask, return on investment and exit strategy being a few things to consider.

As an advisor to not-for-profits and charities, what advice do you have?

Make sure you have the expertise in house (on the team or on the advisory board) with someone who is experienced in applying for grants. If you are doing it cold, someone who has done it before can really give you insights into what you should and shouldn't be saying, and ease the process. Especially with a charity, you must maintain your integrity and stay transparent throughout.

At what point should a founder put their hand up and say this isn't working?

Give yourself six months, follow your gut and ask trusted advisors. If you are road-mapping, you always have something to benchmark against and you can therefore keep track of the plan, to see where you are, where you need to be and where you can actually go.

Before you start your entrepreneurial journey, what would you want to know?

How to set yourself up for success with investors. If you start your business with the right documents, planning and due diligence, this will make you investor-ready when the time comes. Many startups and entrepreneurs delay their investment process because they don't focus on documentation as a fundamental part of running a business. Start taking note of impact, financial growth and customer satisfaction from the start.

What is your advice for those who are unprepared for entrepreneurship?

It's probably as much of a life lesson as a financial one, but make sure there's chemistry and trust with the people you are working with. As a founder, investor and advisor I have found that working with people who connect and understand one another has led to healthier and more fruitful working relationships than those who haven't. Money makes the world go round, so you have to be careful with who you're taking on that journey.

Afterthoughts

As a first-time founder, the world of business seems fun but the financial side stressful. Devina's advice reminds us to plan for the future, find purpose in the business before growth and present our successes to our network. Through this, you can generate brand awareness and support, if you choose to go down the investment route. Her advice seems simple but, in reality, can be the difference between financial failure and financial security. She echoes the comments we've discussed in this chapter already: ensure you have enough runway to keep you afloat for six months, ask for help when required and go back to your financial models to stay on track.

EXERCISE

Shifting your money mindset is fundamental to managing your finances as an entrepreneur. Taking into account what we have learnt in this chapter, sit down with your team and brainstorm the current finances and future projected finances. Start working towards building your own financial sheets and tools that can support your business growth and sustain long-term revenue.

WORKBOOK

_____

_____

_____

_____

_____

_____

_____

_____

_____

_____

_____

_____

_____

_____

_____

_____

_____

_____

_____

_____

_____

_____

_____

CHAPTER TEN

How to influence people and win clients

Business leaders inspire others to do what they're doing and keep going. They set themselves apart from the average person by taking responsibility for leading the way. Being an entrepreneur involves solving problems, storytelling and convincing others that your business is the best solution for them.

At this stage, you have a brand, a business and boss status. The foundations seem strong, so now we start building the house.

In the last chapter, we spoke about finances and money management. In this chapter, we will be focusing on money through a different lens. Rather than focusing on how to manage it, let's discuss how to carry on generating it. A large part of your success will be determined by your sales technique.

Influencing is a skill I didn't understand until the business required it in order to grow and generate additional revenue streams. Today, I spend more time talking and pitching the business to potential clients than I do anything else. Marketing is part of influencing new business but so is your presence and influence as a business leader.

What does it mean to influence people?

Influencing is the power to convince someone to change their behaviour, perspective or decision.

Having met hundreds of entrepreneurs since starting my journey and this book, here are the five common traits I believe make entrepreneurs great influencers:

1 **Hunger** to build something. Entrepreneurs don't need to be visibly hungry. They do however need to be more determined to make things work!
2 A true **passion** for their vision even if others don't believe. Entrepreneurs aren't ones to veer away at the first hurdle; their energy keeps them aligned and going.
3 **Authenticity** in their approach, with or without people around. Influencers need to be true to their mission otherwise their audience will see right through them.
4 The ability to **care** and consider the feelings, approaches and suggestions of others. A working business has many parts, and it's up to the entrepreneur and business founder to find the matching pieces and encourage them to fit together.
5 **Unreasonable expectations** and standards from yourself and the rest of the world. An entrepreneur is someone who sees more than what is already there, who builds on content and businesses that already exist but adds their vision – and isn't afraid to challenge the status quo.
6 A **great leader** (which we covered in Chapter 7) has to have empathy, vision and confidence.

Entrepreneurs are often the face of their business and the main point of contact. Learning the art of influencing people and being a great business leader is what will set you up for success.

Ways to build influential relationships

Influencing isn't an overnight process. It requires consistency and relationship building. It's important to update your LinkedIn profile with success stories and testimonials. It's the trust, truth and reliability that wins people over.

1 The first step is to **identify** what or who you would like to influence and why. You need to be clear on what you want and be able to articulate that reasoning.

2 The second step is to build **trust**. Influencing requires trust and building relationships with new people. Influencing increases business awareness and generates new revenue streams and opportunities. This may take time. One way to establish trust is to ask someone how you can help them and deliver on that task.

3 The last step is to **listen**. Active listening is the act of consciously listening to what others are saying and hearing their words without interpreting them to serve your own purpose. Often, we mistake listening for hearing what we want to hear and misinterpret the conversation. Once you listen to the person, hear what they want, you can go back with questions, thoughts and suggestions.

There are a few types of influencer. Social media influencers are spokespersons for a brand or organization, normally in a paid capacity. Influential entrepreneurs are not paid for their work but are seen as the spokesperson for the business. Entrepreneurs and business owners can be social media influencers.

Influencing people can open you up to scrutiny and criticism in a way that might not have been possible before, especially in this digital age. Knowing that it's much easier for consumers to find you and information about you online means that you must also consider your presence, perception and partnerships. I believe that this same thought process can be used to take a step back and reflect on the internal business values — how you want people to feel about yourself and the business model. For entrepreneurs, this means knowing what you stand for, understanding how each and every element of your supply chain works and ensuring that you meet the values you have set for yourself.

This scrutiny can be intimidating at first, but it's also a good reminder to make sure you keep your business ethical. Every moment is an opportunity to pitch yourself and your business. You never know who's in the room listening. What this means is that you must always be ready with the right material to stand out from the crowd.

What is a pitch?

A pitch is a brief presentation given to one or more people, usually in person, but sometimes virtually. The famous '30-second elevator pitch' is a short, snappy summary of your business with a clear call to action.

What are the five types of pitches?

1 **Investor** – the pitch is one where you are trying to raise money or gain investment. This style of pitch requires a story with a clear problem, solution and action. You'll include details that make the business seem as compelling as possible, like the total addressable market, competitors and any proven metrics of success. Ultimately, you are reassuring and exciting the investor to believe in your business and invest in your vision.

2 **Customers** – your customer already exists, so this is about how to make their experience better and ensure their loyalty. This style of pitch may be more conversational in approach, asking for feedback and encouraging conversation. You might set up a call with a different customer each week, or send out a survey. Ultimately, you are reminding the customer why they love your business.

3 **Sales** – this pitch is one where you are trying to grow your market share or size. In this pitch, you are selling yourself to a potential future customer and generating value. There is a

wide range of ways to do this, from asking for emails in exchange for a PDF of research, to posting Instagram advertisements. Ultimately, you are educating and attracting a potential customer.

4 **Employees** – this pitch is one where you are trying to recruit and grow your business. Business relationships are a two-way street. Like any relationship, it should work for both you and them. This style of pitch must be like a conversation, encouraging the other person to agree with your vision and reminding them that they are an asset. This gets easier as your company grows bigger. Ultimately, you are exciting and inspiring a future employee.

5 **Partners** – the hardest of them all I believe, because in my experience these can take years to develop and build on before they go through. This pitch is one where you are focused on the partner company and how your business can provide them with a solution, impact their strategy or enhance their brand. Partner pitches require you to go the extra mile to find the best person to talk to, convince them that your business will make their life better and persuade them to sign on the dotted line. Ultimately, you are problem-solving and exciting a future partner.

Why is finessing a pitch important?

Pitching yourself, your brand and business takes time and practice. I have pitched myself successfully through a LinkedIn comment that converted into a paid training session, and simultaneously flunked a three-minute pitch when dealing with potential partners. Flunking a pitch isn't uncommon – the more founders I meet, the more I learn it's an essential part of business. It's how you finesse your pitch from that failure that makes the difference between you and another.

All good pitches have a few things in common: they should be time-bound, specific and with a clear call to action. People like to buy into people who are positively passionate about what they are doing. If you aren't able to pitch yourself and promote your business, then who will?

The pitch deck

A pitch deck is a brief written presentation or document, often created using PowerPoint, Keynote or Prezi, and provides your audience with a quick overview of your business plan. You usually use your pitch deck during face-to-face or online meetings with potential investors, customers, partners and co-founders.

A standard pitch deck should have no more than 15 slides, according to Janelle Tam (nd) from Y Combinator. The objective is to communicate your business proposition in a simple PowerPoint-style presentation. Your deck should include:

1 **Executive summary** – top-line details including business name, vision, mission, growth plans and your call to action.
2 **Company introduction and mission statement** – the one-liner that defines you.
3 **Problem** – What is the bigger problem? What need isn't being met? How is the customer feeling, handling, coping?
4 **Solution** – your value proposition (see Chapter 3). If you have a minimum viable product (MVP) or case studies, include these to make it more compelling.
5 **Why now?** – How has the industry changed over time? Why is this solution important? Why are you the best business for the job?
6 **Market size** – What is the total market size and, of that total, what percentage are you specifically targeting? This can also include current traction or projected road map.
7 **Product** – the what and why of your business.

8 **Team** – yourself, the team, advisors and board members.
9 **Business model** – How much money will you make? What will the price of each product or service be? How do you plan on acquiring and retaining customers? (See Chapter 3.)
10 **Competition** – Who are your competitors? How do they stack up against your proposition?
11 **Financials** – What are your revenue projections? Market penetration and operation costs? (See Chapter 9.)
12 **The ask and exit** – if this is a pitch for investors, they're waiting for your call to action and ultimately information on how you plan to grow their initial investment when the time comes to sell or pay equity. What are you wanting from investors? How can they support your vision? What is the exit strategy for them?
13 **The business's contact page** – this should include your social media links and email address.

If you have a demonstration of your business product or service, feel free to add this in as it can add more substance to the conversation. Remember that each slide should have only one main point to relay to the end user.

What makes a good pitch deck?

Your pitch deck should be clean, neat and accessible. Keep all fonts and colours similar to those of your brand, use high-quality photos and ensure your information slides complement each other and your conversation.

I asked June Angelides MBE, banker turned entrepreneur turned early-stage tech investor for Samos and Debut Sessions, what makes a good pitch. She shared that 'a great pitch takes an investor on a journey, helping them to understand why you are the best person to be building this business. What the investors are really looking to understand is how you are going to weather the bumps along the way, because there will be many.'

The written pitch

The written pitch is getting your business idea and proposition down on paper (or email). This is the hardest pitch, as it can take seconds to read and a lifetime of crafting. If you consider the number of messages your potential client receives daily, what makes yours stand out from the rest? I recommend the following structure:

1 **Introduce** the idea and business – define your angle and USP.
2 **Explain** why your business idea is timely and important – relate it to current-day events, or other relevant headlines.
3 **Consider** how you can solve their problem or meet their needs – this can be through something you've seen that was written by the end user, a problem defined in the media or a recent report you have read.
4 **Contact** details – share how someone can get in touch with you.
5 **Link** your website – ensure that there is a website link in case they'd like more information.

Here is an example of a written pitch that has won me business in the past:

> Hi _____ I have seen that your company is serious about diversity and inclusion this year, especially getting womxn into the industry. At LMF Network we are launching our second global mentoring programme to encourage mobility in technology and digital. From our pilot, we know that 70 per cent of participants identified as womxn from BAME backgrounds, 89 per cent of participants are more likely to apply for a role if companies are involved as mentors or lead the sessions, and 93 per cent suggested that this programme provided them with greater confidence in their capabilities. Given that this is strategically important to the growth of your organization, I was hoping you'd be interested in getting

involved as a partner organization or mentoring partner? I am free on Thursday at 3 pm for a 15-minute call if you are? If so, please let me know and I can send over an invite, or here is my email for further comms: hello@lmfnetwork.com. I have attached our most recent blog on the mentoring programme for further information.

Templates that you can use

Hello _____ – hope you are well. My name is _____ and I have seen your journey from A to B, which is very impressive. I have seen your most recent post on _____ and found this of interest because _____. If you have 15 minutes this week, I'd like to schedule an introduction with you to discuss _____. If not, please send across an email and I can forward some more information. Thank you for your time.

Hello _____ – hope the week is going well. I wanted to drop a quick note to discuss _____ as I can see it's something of interest to you and the business. Through my own business, I have been working on _____ and have successfully _____. If you have 15 minutes on Wednesday at noon, I would appreciate the opportunity to talk you through it, otherwise I can send further information by email. Thank you.

Hello _____. I can see that you are looking for a speaker with experience in diversity, business and entrepreneurship. I have recently written a book titled *Unprepared to Entrepreneur*, which covers all aspects of entrepreneurship. Furthermore, I am a trained speaker, having delivered presentations to the likes of *Financial Times*, Barclays and King. I am interested in the opportunity and would appreciate an email address to send further information. You can also see additional information on my website (insert link). Look forward to hearing from you.

In-person pitching

This kind of pitch should be subtle and relaxed, highlighting who you are, what your business can do and how someone else can get involved. You should aim to make your in-person pitch somewhere between 30 seconds and two minutes long.

Here is a sample structure you can use:

- **Begin with inspiration** – explain your motivation for building the product. This might be a deep love for the product category, a bad experience with a similar product, or a random moment of inspiration. Keep your target audience in mind!
- **Introduce your business problem, solution and USP** – walk the participant through your initial problem, solution and market difference, as discussed in Chapters 2 and 3.
- **Bring in your team story** – Why do you care so much about this design? What's your background? The more that someone empathizes with your story, the more they'll want to join your community or buy from you.
- **End with a clear call to action** – let them know exactly how they can help to elevate your brand or business.

And then what?

Remember to follow up! At the beginning of my journey, I would forget, or not prioritize follow-ups, recommendations and re-engagement. Although there is the possibility your prospective client isn't getting back because they are simply busy or the timing isn't right, the most plausible reason is that they haven't remembered all the details you initially pitched.

For each message or pitch, follow up one week later, two weeks later and a month later. Add reminders in your calendar to 'get back in touch' or enable the syncing of CRM tools to ensure that they're on your list. If you are pestering a potential client, they will let you know. However, as they say in advertising, it takes around three attempts before someone notices you.

Alyssa Ordu, freelance marketing, diversity & inclusion consultant, says 'email outreach is a powerful and cheap tool. And when we get it right, it doesn't have to feel 'cold' at all... I have seen first hand just how far we can leverage it to make connections/network, drive sales and raise awareness. In this connected life, we're (more often than not) only an email away from anyone. In the world!' In her experience, 'people are smart, they know when they're being sold to, they don't like it, and therefore don't engage with generic emails. So before you send that template email – get clear on your why, do your research to understand what is important to the person/company you're outreaching (based on their digital footprints) and get specific about the ask or offer and how it benefits them.'

The trick, as with anything, is practice. The first few times you will get it wrong. However, you need to make these mistakes to know what's relevant and what's rubbish. Each entrepreneur brings their unique style of writing and tone to the table, so there's no right or wrong way to do it, as long as you ensure you are clear and concise.

How do you convert prospects into clients?

To ensure the desired outcome, let's break down the steps required to win a project.

Kim Darragon, founder of Kim Does Marketing, a marketing consultancy for small businesses and startups, tells me that her website is 'fully optimized with the right information to boost conversion rates' such as the services she provides, case studies, new client testimonials and press features that demonstrate expertise. As a small business owner, she shares that 'potential clients will ultimately look at my website to fill out the contact form and get in touch. Once I have received their query, I reply in less than 24 hours with a bespoke answer with some initial guidance on how to approach their challenges.' I ask her how she converts new business into potential clients, to which Kim shares that she 'suggests a 20-minute discovery call, which is a great way to listen and understand their needs, showcase my expertise in a friendly way and build trust. It's all about being detailed, personalized and trustworthy from the start.' As an entrepreneur you can find yourself juggling a number of prospective clients. By using these techniques, Kim is able to showcase her area of specialization while managing her customer queries in a practical way.

Five ways to secure new business

1 **Cold calls/emails** – contacting individuals you don't know personally or those who have not expressed interest in the business before, who you believe might be helpful for your business. This is a traditional sales move that involves researching companies, adding all contact information to a tracking tool, emailing or calling with your pitches, and logging next steps.

2 **Networking** – introducing yourself to individuals through any medium or forum is a good way to start conversations. One of the things I most look forward to as an entrepreneur is the opportunity to network to see how we can work together. This approach to new business often requires deep relationship building, consistent communication and co-creating a solution.

3 **Ask for referrals** – ask previous clients to refer you to a friend or colleague. Eighty-five per cent of opportunities come through referrals, according to Christina Vukova (2021), in an article for *Review 42*, so this is a good way to kick off that conversation. This approach to new business may seem like a favour or gesture in kind, so an expectation to return the referral might be suggested.

4 **Content creation and leveraging social media** – I'm a big fan of using social media to generate new business. As discussed in previous chapters, I often share content that self-promotes my activities. Chop and rework content into digestible nuggets with clear calls to action. Useful, engaging and regular content can validate your offering in people's minds and this can bring opportunities to you rather than you having to try to win these opportunities.

5 **Newsletters** – engage and educate your audience through newsletters. Building and maintaining an email list takes effort, but pays off. Some companies use their email lists to create specific, targeted campaigns, for example. Eighty-one per cent of B2B marketers say their most-used form of content marketing is newsletters, according to the Content Marketing Institute (2020).

Jaz Broughton, Career and Life Coach, tells me that she uses social media as a tool for outreach, not for fun. She details her process when pitching to clients: 'Content > Call to action > Genuine communication > Invitation is usually the flow regardless of platform', and expands on that, saying 'it's an invitation, not an obligation. So I always leave room for them to respond with a no and for us to stay connected without awkwardness. I also never show up empty-handed; there is a service, event, workshop, podcast episode or answers to their questions shared in the interaction.'

Following on from Jaz's advice, I would add: don't be afraid of connecting with someone over multiple platforms, or at least three times. I know that life, work and emails can sometimes become overwhelming, and so if someone hasn't replied, it's not because they're not interested but because they may be busy.

The reality of being ghosted

The unfortunate truth is that people may ghost you despite having started the conversation. If you are unaware of this term, ghosting is being avoided and ignored.

In some cases, it's when a message has been sent, you've seen the blue tick and gained no reply. In other cases, it's a client taking you out for a business meeting, promising you that the work is yours and never replying to further communications.

If you are being ghosted or have been ghosted, here are three ways in which you can re-boost that conversation:

1 Hey _____. I hope you are well. I would like to pick this back up at a time convenient to you. Shall we organize a meeting next week to discuss how to move forward?
2 Hey _____. We spoke last year regarding an opportunity to work together. The time wasn't right back then, but I would like to pick this back up to see if we can collaborate in the near future.
3 Hey _____. I hope you are doing well. I read this article and thought it may be of interest to you, as when we last spoke we were discussing _____. It would be great to hear more about what you are currently working on and how (insert business name) can support you. Do you have 15 minutes this month for a catch-up?

Life happens, sometimes we miss an email – other times we flunk on commitments because of uncertainty. Whatever the reason, don't be afraid to get back in touch and follow up on the conversation. And if someone doesn't respond despite persistent reaching out, let them go. Some opportunities are not meant to be.

What is your measure of success?

While seeking and securing new business, always remember to go back to your core values, reasons why and measure of success. I found my first year of entrepreneurship difficult when I was offered this book deal. From a business perspective, balancing two new businesses with a book (which generated no immediate income) was difficult. I remember taking a step back around

February 2021, which meant going into my calendar and rescheduling or declining all conversations that weren't prioritizing current business, social impact or getting the book written. I paused all focus on new business and re-evaluated my measure of success as not purely monetary, but as time to think, moments to write and people to upskill.

CASE STUDY   Deborah Okenla

Deborah Okenla is an angel investor, advisor, founder and CEO of Your Startup, Your Story (YSYS), an organization providing employment and entrepreneurship opportunities for diverse talent in technology. Since 2017 they have provided access to opportunities for over 10,000 individuals across the UK, partnering with organizations such as FT, Mayor of London, LinkedIn, JPMorgan, Niantic and Atomico. She has been named as one of *Computer Weekly's* Most Influential Women in Tech Rising Stars of 2020, and listed in the UK's Top 100 Black and Minority Ethnic Leaders in Technology by the FT in 2018 and 2019. Deborah sits on the advisory board for AND Digital, Coders of Colour, the No.10 Innovation Fellowship Programme and DCMS.

You started as a WhatsApp community – how did you convince people to join?

The WhatsApp community was originally created for people in technology to lean on one another for support. This was late 2016, when in my personal experience little was being done to support ethnic minorities in the technology space. Initially, I invited my own friends and those I had met through my professional work. The conversations would be of quality, discussing topics from career progression and salary negotiation to future startup ideas. I was there to facilitate and probe the conversation, which many welcomed as it meant they could answer freely. Slowly, those in the group started to invite their own friends and network. Eventually, the group itself got too big for WhatsApp so I had to move over to Slack. This was a tricky move, as I knew we may lose some people, especially as Slack was a new tool back then. To combat this, every Friday I hosted a meetup in a central location to bring community members together and teach them how to use Slack. This effort and education are what others tell me they enjoyed and hence, I was able to influence people by bringing them on the journey and sharing my knowledge to upskill. This became the values of YSYS.

How did you get over your initial fear of pitching yourself and the business?

Our first pitch was terrifying, as I had never pitched before and I was unprepared for the consequences. Tapping into what I had learnt working for technology companies such as Huckletree and Google, I created the first decks, which told the story of YSYS, the problem we were solving and why companies should work with us. The initial draft I sent to some people in my network whose opinions I trusted. The feedback was welcomed, as I inevitably wanted to win the contract and they wanted to support. I also practiced my pitch – through video recordings, conversations with friends and leaning into my authentic voice rather than trying to be someone else.

What would you have done differently?

Winning new business is a process. I would have outlined the steps, from creating the initial pitch, to communicating the message, to following up, so that I was aware of the work and then asked for more money. What I have learnt is that someone isn't paying you for your current service, but for your experience, community and knowledge. I hadn't been working for many years, but I had tapped into a community of different people, had lived experiences as a black woman in tech and understood the problems for entrepreneurs in their initial startup phase. These are selling points, benefits and USPs that only I can offer – and what sets me apart from competitors.

How important is it as an entrepreneur to influence and promote your business?

If you don't live and breathe your business, talk about it through your work and show successes – who will? Being an introvert, I don't spend as much time as I should elevating my own personal brand but do focus on amplifying my business. I believe that your actions will come full circle and so YSYS has received accolades, awards and recognition – which ultimately spotlights my team and myself. These actions, services and achievements (through case studies, press and referrals) have helped me to grow the business in a short period of time. I therefore think it's very important to be seen as influential and promote your business, because that will generate new business and allow you to sustain growth.

Have you ever been ghosted or ghosted someone? How did you reignite the conversation?

Unfortunately, sometimes this happens for a number of reasons, ranging from your inbox being full, to your workload being busy, to people forgetting. I tend to give other people the benefit of the doubt, so I follow up after a couple of weeks asking if they're okay and still interested in the opportunity to work together. A good tip is to include a recent article, podcast or weblink that may interest them, so it's not direct sales but informative.

When it comes to winning clients, what key advice do you want to give new entrepreneurs?

Clients, customers and consumers are all interested in two things: how you will solve their problem, and your relationship with them. Every three months at YSYS we send an update email or report to our current, past and future clients. Take care of your clients – this can be checking in when you haven't spoken, retweeting their tweets or sending presents to end the year. For our fourth birthday in 2021, we sent clients cupcakes to say thank you, along with a digital copy of our Impact Report (2020–2021). Small gestures, whether that's remembering their last conversation, asking about their day or checking in, go a long way! Business is also personal, because you're interacting with another person (not a robot).

Afterthoughts

Once your business is in full flow, the real challenge is sustaining your growth with new business, clients and partners. The most frustrating thing as an entrepreneur is questioning why others aren't as passionate about your business as you are. At the start, pitching and influencing people seemed like an easy task but that was because I underestimated the technique and time it would take. Deborah's story is helpful because she tells us that as founders, if we don't feel comfortable sharing our own individual brand, we can still share the great work our business is doing and invite partners to get involved, to our mutual benefit. Starting a conversation isn't the hard part, but articulating the message so it captures their attention is what differentiates you from any other business in starting a working relationship. The great thing about influencing and winning clients is that the skills can be learnt and each entrepreneur is able to bring their personal touch – which is what makes the conversation unique and authentic. Remember, you don't have to be someone else when sending the message, but the message needs to add value – read, pitched or in person.

WORKBOOK

_____

_____

_____

_____

_____

_____

_____

_____

_____

_____

_____

_____

_____

_____

_____

_____

_____

_____

_____

_____

_____

_____

Eleven methods to the madness of starting your own business

When I started writing this book I was completely out of my depth. At the start, I constantly told my editor that I wasn't sure how I would write the whole book and yet somehow, the week before submission I was 13,000 words over, with a lot left to say. The point is, you never know what you can do until you give it a go. I scheduled writing sessions, used my phone to record random thoughts I had and gave it my best shot.

It's the same with entrepreneurship – small steps and being outside of your comfort zone is where you will grow. In a similar respect, the method to the entrepreneurial madness evolves. The discussion points I have shared, entrepreneurs I have learnt from and the exercises I have undertaken have helped me to finesse my businesses in the same way as they can for you.

For the final chapter, I wanted to share my reflections on topics that we weren't able to cover in depth but are fundamental in preparing yourself as an entrepreneur.

My story isn't unique, but that's the point.

I am the first-generation immigrant child to Pakistani parents and arrived in the UK a few weeks before my fifth birthday. Half of my life was spent growing up on a council estate. I have vivid memories of having to manage money, expectations and even wants because we had limited disposable funds. While other children's parents shopped at the likes of Marks & Spencer and Waitrose, we enjoyed the aisles of Tesco and Lidl. My parents didn't have university degrees or wealth or business experience, but hustled hard to provide a stable home for four children and give them a brilliant upbringing. It's through these adventures that I first learnt and saw hustle culture for what it truly meant for those who had no other choice – and remember these stories when I find myself unsure of what the next move is.

This book will be published around my 29th birthday. If you told my 19-year-old self I would be building this entrepreneurial life, achieving regular accolades and living what I believe are my dreams, she wouldn't have believed you. And yet, here I am, more ambitious than ever before.

I hope, through the teachings of this book, you too can become the boss you want to be and build the life you want.

1 Small wins give you the confidence to try something bigger

Given that much of this took place before and during the COVID-19 pandemic, my greatest takeaway is to not plan too far ahead, because you never know what will happen tomorrow. For this reason, I recommend setting goals for 18–24 months and working through the milestones you need to achieve them. It's awesome to have a bigger vision, but don't get too caught up with it and forget to celebrate the smaller wins. The fact you have stuck it out, read this book through to the end and even tried a few exercises is a win that will give you the confidence to do something bigger. That something bigger is the best way to find yourself, finesse your business and carry on strengthening your entrepreneurial muscles.

2 You don't need the title or accolades

At the end of 2020, I was nominated for a *Forbes* 30 Under 30 award. By February 2021, I was shortlisted and invited to send in my headshot. It sounds naive, but at that moment I was convinced I was going to be one of the winners. On 8 April 2021, the list for Europe was released – and I wasn't on it. If I am being very honest, it hurt. I found myself drowning my sorrows in a few cups of tea and cancelling all my meetings. Ironically, it reminded me of a similar experience when I was applying for university graduate schemes. In 2014, I was invited to a final informal interview round for Ernst & Young in London. I walked in, wearing a purple dress and black boots, thinking that I had them in the bag. I walked out one hour later, embarrassed and with no offer and no contract. Though the rejection made me sad, it allowed me to explore new and other options.

On that same afternoon, after allowing myself a few hours to feel all the emotions, I read through the *Forbes* winners and well, of course, they deserved it. I posted my thoughts on LinkedIn, congratulating the winners but also sharing that I had missed out. To my surprise, I received a handful of messages from industry leaders telling me the message was powerful and they too missed out. On reflection, maybe I needed this to humble my business self, remind me that some things don't go to plan and it's what you do after that counts. Not being on a list of winners or receiving that title doesn't make you less of an entrepreneur. It's merely another way to add credibility. Your preparation for entrepreneurship and what you do in practice is not defined by a list or title, but by the impact you are creating.

3 Productive procrastination is the key to productivity

As mentioned above, I found writing a book very difficult and at times exhausting. I am not a natural writer – put me in front of 1,000 people and I can speak; ask me to write 1,000 words and I have writer's block. Through these moments, I realized that I am a serial procrastinator.

I found myself drifting from the now to the what if – what then – what's happening? I caught myself randomly picking up my phone to avoid work and scrolling aimlessly through social media. There were regular instances where I would check my emails at 3 am, fearing I had missed an opportunity, but deny my inbox the same level of focus during the day.

It took a serious conversation with myself to understand what was happening. Through a reflective exercise focused on self-awareness, I admitted to some serious truths about my working style. Though at times I can be super focused, I have poor organizational skills, tend to fidget and am easily distracted by other tasks. I take on more work as a way to ignore what is already on my plate. This new-found sense of reality has helped me to become productive in my own way, with my own definition of what it means for my work.

For example, one day I decided to leave my phone in the living room and challenged myself to stick to the to-do list I had made earlier in the day. The list didn't only include work-related tasks, but life tasks such as checking in on friends and organizing my kitchen cupboards. Any time I would find myself procrastinating, I would jump onto a task of lower priority. Using this technique, I have balanced running a household with running two full-time businesses; doing the grocery shopping, making dinner and cleaning the house while replying to emails, sending proposals and managing clients.

Having realized this worked for me, I coined the term 'productive procrastination'. Excited by this new idea, I started researching on the internet to understand if this was a real concept or one I had created. Turns out, I wasn't the founder of this school of thought but it's a new area that is still yet to be further explored.

Productive procrastination is not a new term but one that I hadn't heard of before. According to *Kanban Zone* (Leal, 2020), productive procrastination is 'a process that some people use to help them manage their thoughts and emotions towards completing their pending tasks. Some people tend to view procrastination in a negative light, but when done properly, procrastination can actually be a healthy way of dealing with your to-do list.' I found myself being one of those people.

If you find yourself wandering, here's a method that you can try:

- Write a list of things you need to get done, at work, at home and in your life.
- Prioritize them into high, medium and low. Naturally, start with the high and work your way through to the medium.
- When you feel you are drifting or procrastinating, turn to the lower tasks and tick them off.

Other ways in which you can productively procrastinate include:

- maintaining a healthy lifestyle, eg cooking a new dish, going on a walk;
- reading work-related content, eg academic articles on topics of interest or what are the new trends in your industry;
- growing your personal brand, eg creating a TikTok video, writing a blog or finessing Instagram content.

Since a young child, I've viewed the idea of being a procrastinator as a negative. However, each entrepreneur has a method to their own madness and it turns out that procrastination is one of mine. Using this technique, I was able to balance two businesses, a book and the stresses that come with life, switching from one version of me to another while keeping productive.

4 Becoming a boss can be stressful for relationships, romance and love

As an entrepreneur, you can't help but get caught up in your vision and at times can forget yourself and others around you. At the same time as securing this book deal, I got married. It's not something I shared on social media or presented to the world, because I didn't think it was relevant to my story or to my work. For my own sanity, I found separating the two worlds incredibly healthy. Since becoming an entrepreneur, many of my conversations with other businesspeople over coffee have ended up being about life, love and romance. I like to keep them separate but the two worlds do tend to overlap organically. As a business person, your business becomes your life because you don't have anything else to fall back on. For this reason, I believe it's important to share your whys with your loved ones, bring them into your mission and remind them of why running your business is important for you. Use them as a sounding board, but don't allow their opinion to sway you or your business's trajectory – remember it's your mission. When and if dating, listen to the other person but also educate them on what you are doing. When married, invite your partner to discuss their working day at the dinner table, and if single, call friends and organize a dinner party. Always remember that discussing what is on your mind is a form of self-care. Remember to give yourself the time to love yourself and make self-care a priority (as discussed in Chapter 8). This may be as simple as taking a 30-minute break each day without any technology and making sure you close your work laptop at a decent time on a Friday night.

5 If you stop enjoying entrepreneurship, you're exhausted

After 12 months of running my own business, filing taxes and wearing many hats, I found myself exhausted. One thing I have learnt through entrepreneurship is to share your feelings and thoughts – so I did. Turns out, I wasn't the only one! Feeling exhausted is a natural part of entrepreneurship – you may even stop enjoying your business altogether. This isn't a reflection on the state of the business as much as it is a reflection on you. If you are not enjoying your current venture, consider this may be because you don't feel passionate about the business any more. You may not be the best person to lead the idea forward or you may need more help.

In my case, it was because I was so adamant about trying to be the best in everything that at times I wasn't able to balance the various business tasks I was undertaking. Additionally, I would start new tasks and say yes to doing things way before finishing the previous task.

By April 2021 I was exhausted and stopped enjoying the life of an entrepreneur. For a second, I thought 'wouldn't it be nice to play it safe – have a nine to five and know exactly what your daily tasks are'. That thought didn't last long, but what it did do was bring forward the reality that I hadn't taken a day off in 18 months. I shared this with my business friends and the remedy was simple – stop, delegate and take time off. I know it's simple in reality but in practice it can be very difficult, so from that moment I decided that every quarter I would take a week off to enjoy everything that wasn't business-related and focus on trying new things. Some things on my list include pottery making, running a half marathon and knitting.

6 Define your measure of success, not somebody else's

A not-so-great part of being an entrepreneur is that you are benchmarked against other people who are doing the same thing, or a similar thing to you. Though it's interesting to know where you are, the problem comes when you are comparing not effort and foundations but surface-value wins. By this, I mean awards, funding and investment. As a social entrepreneur, I must admit that I have faced my own version of discrimination because many organizations still don't consider the style of my business sustainable. I was turned down for a guest lecturing opportunity because my business had not gained venture capital funding or been around for 10 years plus. It bothered me to not be considered an 'entrepreneur' because I didn't fit that box or label. However, in the grand scheme of things, that isn't important any more – the measure of success comes from you and your reporting, not from the outside world. My measure of success is driven by impact: upskilling, which leads to progression and repeat business. It's easy to get caught up in the hype of comparison and success but remember – you have started, that's the biggest hurdle of all – the rest is maintaining your measure of success and levelling up as you evolve.

7 Prepare to practise, not to perfect

Entrepreneurship, running a business, becoming a founder, managing a team, handling a difficult conversation, even letting someone go; these aren't skills we are born with. They are skills that are learnt. In the same way we have spoken about continuously improving our business, we must continuously improve ourselves. The best way to do that is to practise. In reality, there are very few things that you will get right the first time, so why not give yourself a fair chance to figure it out, get things wrong and try again? If we wait around for the 'perfect time', a good time may have passed and an opportunity gone. If we think about the opportunity cost, it's not worth losing something because you want it to be perfect – in practice, nothing ever is. Preparing yourself to be an entrepreneur is equivalent to preparing yourself to fail, figure it out and try again.

8 Not all passion projects need to become a multi-million-pound business

Throughout this book you have heard the story of the LMF Network. We have grown in a way I never expected and completely outgrown our original vision of a brunch club. When writing this book and sharing activities, I decided to redo our own business model. Despite COVID-19, we ended our year with triple the turnover we expected in the bank thanks to donations, sponsorships and partnerships. Most of this money was spent running and maintaining the mentoring programme, buying technical software and compensating the team. To recap, in February 2021, we launched the UK's largest mentoring programme with 600 participants across 14 countries, of whom 90 per cent identified as women and non-binary. By March, we had released four diversity research papers to explore inclusive topics that were necessary for our services. Despite these efforts, our advisory board stepped down after serving for 18 months and our income froze. At this point, I went back to the drawing board and made the decision to transition into a charitable organization. Because of the COVID-19 pandemic and budget constraints, it was becoming harder to close investment from businesses and convince them to support our mission. The charitable process is longer than any other, as there's thorough due diligence after the application process. By the time this book comes out, you will have heard about our journey – 'brunch to social good business'. All things considered, it's better to know what does and doesn't work early on so that you can thrive strategically in the long run.

9 Let your personal brand do the talking

At the same time as launching the network full time, I was forced to start my own commercial business. I use the word 'forced' because the financial odds were stacked against me given that I had launched a CIC right before the COVID-19 pandemic struck, and had no financial support from the UK government. In reality, this was the best decision and one of the greatest achievements, which naturally came from being forced outside of my comfort zone. Despite some initial teething problems, my business turnover was double what I had earned previously working full-time in a corporate role. Ninety per cent of my income was generated through online channels and through my personal branding efforts, evidencing that it does work. I speak about personal branding in great depth throughout the book and how having an online presence is fundamental to success. Personal branding has allowed me to create an online presence associated with my interests and topics of expertise. In 2021, this landed me opportunities with the likes of Monki, Rens, Vapiano and *The Telegraph*, to name a few. My social following grew by 20 per cent month on month and I was even contacted by LinkedIn to deliver a campaign for International Women's Day.

10 If entrepreneurship doesn't work, at least you're employable

I remember a manager once told me that 'I didn't have the skills to become CEO and that I should stop being so ambitious'. For a moment, I guess I believed her. Saying that, if we consistently let others put us down, we won't thrive and become the people we are meant to be. I am a CEO, a founder and an entrepreneur. Founding and growing your own idea takes guts, resilience and leadership skills – the same hustle and grind companies admire and want for themselves. After my first eight months of entrepreneurship, I was being approached by corporate organizations for senior leadership positions. Two months later, I was contacted by a headhunter because a company was considering me as their CEO. It's at that moment I turned to pen and paper and wrote down all the skills I had gained. If entrepreneurship isn't your thing long term, have no fear – articulate your learnings, successes and failures, and show why you're even more employable than you were before.

11 Always ask why and what's next

The great thing about entrepreneurship is that your opportunities are endless – you make your own decisions and control your next move. It's one thing to consider what is best for your business and its revenue, it's another to know that you can take charge of the companies, partnerships and clients you work with. Given this privilege and power, I encourage you to always ask why and what's next. Why are you doing something? Why does it matter? Why will this help you achieve your goals? And what comes after?

When you start thinking about what is next, you are more likely to work backwards and align your steps so you can achieve that milestone quicker. For example, what's next is a talk show – my why is because I want to take this book into a visual and audio format. My next moves are to:

- Launch a live version of strategically winging it (the podcast) in the format of a talk show, using LinkedIn Live and YouTube.
- Apply for a PhD to understand the intersection of gender, ethnicity and workplace attrition.
- Sign up for a 10k run and dedicate myself to this goal.

Your why and what's next don't have to be business related, they can be part of a passion project or new hobby.

CASE STUDY   Edwina Dunn

For my final interview, I had the pleasure of talking to Edwina Dunn, who is the founder of The Female Lead, an educational charity founded to increase the success stories of women. Edwina also founded Starcount and dunnhumby, the company that created Tesco Clubcard. Edwina's entrepreneurial journey started without digital media and now relies on it, so it was interesting to hear her perspective and entrepreneurial evolution. The Female Lead started in 2015 and has since grown to a platform with over 1 million followers.

You are now the founder of three businesses – what made you start and keep going?

If I am being honest, starting a business is similar to childbirth – you remember the good times and the fun, often blocking out the difficult and dire. At the start, entrepreneurship is difficult for everyone because you're figuring out yourself, your business and being told no. The beginning is nothing like the middle or the end, but that's why so many people talk about entrepreneurs not being the ones who are leading the big businesses – you have to change your mindset and be a different person from who you were at the start. In the beginning, you are a phone caller – you do all the jobs – whatever it takes. And in the end, people applaud your successes. It is quite strange – but that feeling of identifying a problem, finding a solution and seeing it work – that adrenaline is what keeps you going.

Why did you start The Female Lead?

I had the experience of running businesses to make money and profits – I wanted to try something new, fresh and fun. Running The Female Lead, which is a registered charity, is fulfilling and a way to give back. When you are doing something and investing your money into something – that's really exciting and helps to shape what you believe in. I wanted to create something to amplify the stories of women and showcase the great work females are doing around the world.

How did you evolve from an innovative entrepreneur to a social entrepreneur?

I started to explore my entrepreneurial style at a time where sexism and discrimination were still at play. I remember a number of moments where I would be presenting to a board of men, who would often turn their heads to one side as I was speaking or not take me seriously. I felt like it was 'ah, she's talking and I must pay attention'. I used to sit in meetings with Clive (my husband), share an original point yet no one would take it. However, Clive would make the same point straight after and they would take it seriously. I remember such experiences making me feel inadequate and frustrated. It was that same frustration that fuelled The Female Lead. My evolution from an innovative entrepreneur to social was because I wanted to enhance fair play. Men aren't better than women and yet things still happen or are done that don't give women space or fairness they deserve. I felt that myself through years of starting and running businesses, and so when the time was right I was asking the question: how do we change that? All of these moments and experiences built up until I had the time to do something about it. A part of being an entrepreneur is being in the right place at the right time with the right people. When I was in the position to do something about it, I didn't want it to be angry or aggressive, but to showcase a wonderful woman doing great things!

Did you ever have an initial pushback for starting an educational charity after launching million-pound businesses?

I wouldn't say pushback, but many did question the why. A very good friend said that she didn't see the point of what I am doing. That comment hurt me, especially because it was right at the start when I was putting it together. However, from experience, I knew that the time had come to do something to support the progression of others, as I had progressed myself into this place of privilege through hard work and effort, no doubt. As an entrepreneur, you build a thick skin and starting every business or something new is exciting! The Female Lead was brand new and a lot more exciting because it was fresh – there were no models, nothing to follow. This meant that I could start from a clean slate to create a vision, mission and business model in the way I wished and invite people to get involved.

How did you balance entrepreneurship with life, identity and family?

It is such a danger to get caught up in one way of doing things. As an entrepreneur, you have started this journey as you have interest, passion and courage – these same traits can be used to manage and balance your personal life. Family help, pull you away and it's enough. You do need to have good people in your life who can say 'enough, you are sounding tense and need a break'. At times it's hard to keep your self-awareness strong because you are so invested in your vision. It's valuable to have people who see you as you and not the title of an entrepreneur, so they can remind you of who you are and support you through the bad times, not only the good. Entrepreneurship can be lonely, cause burnout and sadness. You need to be self-aware, know when to wear and use the parachute. There are so many years where no one notices you or admires you in any way, and accolades or titles aren't important – they add credit but don't make the demands easier.

How do you keep the team motivated?

I have a great team. I am mindful that the team can earn more elsewhere, so it is down to motivation and ensuring they know they belong and their voice matters. I provide the team with the support to create their own path – to be free to do something else. I would recommend leaders listen to their team and their perspectives. Once in a while we get scared, and that's where you really grow – outside of your comfort zone. Give them autonomy such as the scope to present something in a meeting. I never wake up bored and that's the same energy I try to bring to the team. With any person who works, they are in it for something much bigger – thinking about their future self and wondering what did I do, what did my work mean, can it stand the test of time? Will people say 'is this something to be proud of?'

What is your advice for the entrepreneurs of the future?

- You can't recapture the old magic – you have to create new magic.
- You can make what you need to make happen, if you are determined you can find a path.
- People need to be scared, that's motivating.

Afterthoughts

Nothing can quite prepare you for entrepreneurship like living the life of an entrepreneur and learning on the job. Entrepreneurship is an evolutionary process – growing as a person, developing as a business and constantly finding new ways to solve new problems. I started my businesses out of frustration and little did I know that, similar to Edwina's point, that was the greatest motivator of all. Now the business is scaling, I find myself wondering – is it the chase or the completion I enjoy? Often, I believe that entrepreneurs start a business to solve a problem and, in that process, discover a number of different problems to solve. The point is, that as we come to the end of this book, we haven't come to the end of our journey – we've only touched on the beginning. I wish you best of luck in your entrepreneurial endeavours, and believe that you have the toolkit you need to succeed. I can't wait to hear all about your successes (and failures)!

WORKBOOK

_____

_____

_____

_____

_____

_____

_____

_____

_____

_____

_____

_____

_____

_____

_____

_____

_____

_____

_____

_____

_____

_____

_____

_____

_____

References

Chapter 1

Carrick, A (2020) A quarter of women set up their own business due to coronavirus, *CITYA.M.*, 1 September, https://www.cityam.com/a-quarter-of-women-set-up-their-own-business-due-to-coronavirus/ (archived at https://perma.cc/6JQQ-GTQL)

DC Incubator (2019) 60% of new businesses fail in the first 3 years. Here's why, *DC Incubator*, 7 November, https://dcincubator.co.uk/blog/60-of-new-businesses-fail-in-the-first-3-years-heres-why/ (archived at https://perma.cc/MPD6-EZ92)

Duhaime-Ross, A (2014) Apple promised an expansive health app, so why can't I track menstruation? *The Verge*, 25 September, https://www.theverge.com/2014/9/25/6844021/apple-promised-an-expansive-health-app-so-why-cant-i-track (archived at https://perma.cc/MD2M-QJRB)

FSB (2021) UK small business statistics, FSB, https://www.fsb.org.uk/uk-small-business-statistics.html# (archived at https://perma.cc/X2S2-W7AG)

IW Capital (2019) The importance of entrepreneurship to the UK economy, IW Capital, 25 April, https://iwcapital.co.uk/the-importance-of-entrepreneurship-to-the-uk-economy/ (archived at https://perma.cc/L4KT-9M5Q)

Lange *et al* (2019) 2018/2019 United States Report: Global Entrepreneurship Monitor, Babson, https://www.babson.edu/media/babson/assets/blank-center/GEM_USA_2018-2019.pdf?_ga=2.190235563.168691210.1617368253-1763697534.1617368253 (archived at https://perma.cc/MMJ9-LCX5)

Marais, D (2018) How your identity drives your success or failure, *Thrive Global*, 8 March, https://thriveglobal.com/stories/how-your-identity-drives-your-success-or-failure/ (archived at https://perma.cc/2VHR-L5KD)

Numbeo (nd) Cost of living in London, Numbeo, https://www.numbeo.com/cost-of-living/in/London (archived at https://perma.cc/848S-7VRM)

Rosling, L (2020) 64% of Britain's workforce wants to set up their own business, SME Loans, 13 July, https://smeloans.co.uk/blog/64-percent-of-britains-workforce-want-to-start-a-business/ (archived at https://perma.cc/3FAC-TS9H)

Simovic, D (2021) 39 entrepreneur statistics you need to know in 2021, *SmallBizGenius*, 5 January, https://www.smallbizgenius.net/by-the-numbers/entrepreneur-statistics/#gref (archived at https://perma.cc/GN64-AXGW)

Sinek, S (2021) The Golden Circle Presentation, Simon Sinek, https://simonsinek.com/commit/the-golden-circle (archived at https://perma.cc/L3JK-B4DX)

Womanthology (2017) If at first you don't succeed... Why failure was never an option for me as a female tech founder – Melanie Perkins, co-founder and CEO of Canva, *Womanthology*, 28 June, https://www.womanthology.co.uk/first-dont-succeed-failure-never-option-female-tech-founder-melanie-perkins-co-founder-ceo-canva/ (archived at https://perma.cc/K9TT-2S4S)

Chapter 2

Brenner, G (2018) Your brain on creativity: neuroscience research reveals creativity's 'brainprint', *Psychology Today*, 22 February, https://www.psychologytoday.com/gb/blog/experimentations/201802/your-brain-creativity (archived at https://perma.cc/CYA2-MC86)

Cirillo, F (2020) The Pomodoro Technique, Francesco Cirillo, https://francescocirillo.com/pages/pomodoro-technique (archived at https://perma.cc/9GJU-T8E9)

Corazza, G (2014) Creative thinking – how to get out of the box and generate ideas: Giovanni Corazza at TEDxRoma, February, https://www.youtube.com/watch?v=bEusrD8g-dM (archived at https://perma.cc/26F5-Q882)

Maurya, A (2021) What is an unfair advantage? *Ask Leanstack*, http://ask.leanstack.com/en/articles/904720-what-is-an-unfair-advantage (archived at https://perma.cc/2WQJ-BWEW)

Pinchot, G (2017) Four definitions for the intrapreneur, *The Pinchot Perspective*, 30 October, https://www.pinchot.com/2017/10/four-definitions-for-the-intrapreneur.html (archived at https://perma.cc/2A4B-7D3L)

Tseng, J and Poppenk, J (2020) Brain meta-state transitions demarcate thoughts across task contexts exposing the mental noise of trait neuroticism, *Nature Communications*, **11** (1), 3480, pp 1–12

Chapter 3

Bakhshi, S and Gilbert, E (2015) Red, purple and pink: the colors of diffusion on Pinterest, *Plos One*, 6 February, https://journals.plos.org/plosone/article?id=10.1371/journal.pone.0117148# (archived at https://perma.cc/CGT4-Z5BW)

Bridle, J (2018) Opinion: data isn't the new oil – it's the new nuclear power, *IDEAS.TED.COM*, 17 July, https://ideas.ted.com/opinion-data-isnt-the-new-oil-its-the-new-nuclear-power/ (archived at https://perma.cc/28GL-DLCH)

Hastings, R and Meyer, E (2020) *No Rules Rules: Netflix and the culture of reinvention*, Virgin Books, London

Kellner, G (2021) How much is Netflix worth? *GOBankingRates*, 19 March, https://www.gobankingrates.com/money/business/how-much-is-netflix-worth/ (archived at https://perma.cc/4M54-VX57)

Kurt, S and Osueke, K (2014) The effects of color on the moods of college students, *SAGE Open*, **4** (1)

Laja, P (2019) How to create a unique value proposition (with examples), *CXL*, 16 May, https://cxl.com/blog/value-proposition-examples-how-to-create/ (archived at https://perma.cc/DJJ9-2CA8)

Marketplace (2020) CEO Reed Hastings on how Netflix beat Blockbuster, *Marketplace*, 8 September, https://www.marketplace.org/2020/09/08/ceo-reed-hastings-on-how-netflix-beat-blockbuster/ (archived at https://perma.cc/59KA-DPJR)

Shukairy, A (2019) Value proposition: what is it, how it works, and why you should pay attention to it, *Invesp*, 5 June, https://www.invespcro.com/blog/value-proposition-what-is-it-how-it-works-and-why-you-should-pay-attention/ (archived at https://perma.cc/Z43N-5E4M)

Statista (2021) Global digital population as of January 2021, *Statista*, https://www.statista.com/statistics/617136/digital-population-world-wide/ (archived at https://perma.cc/V4QJ-CYBV)

The Chalkboard (2018) In living coral: the meaning behind Pantone's Color Of The Year, *The Chalkboard*, 11 December, https://thechalk-boardmag.com/living-coral-pantone-color-2019 (archived at https://perma.cc/92PA-9NM7)

Twin, A (2020) Value proposition, *Investopedia*, 5 July, https://www.investopedia.com/terms/v/valueproposition.asp (archived at https://perma.cc/63RT-XJBK)

Chapter 4

Chaffey, D and Smith, PR (2017) *Digital Marketing Excellence: Planning, optimizing and integrating online marketing*, 5th edn, Routledge, Abingdon

Dolden, L (2021) Largest virtual mentoring programme launched by charity, *TechRound*, 1 March, https://techround.co.uk/news/largest-virtual-mentoring-programme-launched-by-charity/ (archived at https://perma.cc/95E2-6R62)

Finnis, A (2021) GME share price explained: why GameStop stock value has increased again a month after Reddit 'short squeeze', *inews*, 11 March, https://inews.co.uk/news/business/gme-share-price-gamestop-explained-stock-value-increase-reddit-short-squeeze-905177 (archived at https://perma.cc/7BC9-DQWY)

Influencer Marketing Hub (2021) Clubhouse statistics: revenue, users and more (2021), *Influencer Marketing Hub*, 30 April, https://influencer-marketinghub.com/clubhouse-stats/ (archived at https://perma.cc/76RQ-Y3DA)

Kotler, P (1972) A generic concept of marketing, *Journal of Marketing*, **36** (2), pp 46–54

McCarthy, E J (1971) *Basic Marketing: A managerial approach*, R D Irwin, Homewood, IL

Mediakix (nd) TikTok influencer marketing: the guide to working with TikTok influencers, Mediakix, https://mediakix.com/influencer-market-ing-resources/tik-tok-influencer-marketing/ (archived at https://perma.cc/D6M9-EA4A)

Reitere, S (2021) 10 brands that rule on TikTok, *Socialbakers*, 18 March, https://www.socialbakers.com/blog/brands-that-rule-tiktok (archived at https://perma.cc/2AW9-C4DJ)

Roser, M, Ritchie, H and Ortiz-Ospina, E (2021) Internet, *Our World in Data*, https://ourworldindata.org/internet (archived at https://perma. cc/3X6J-9FJ5)

Statista (2021) Daily time spent on social networking by internet users worldwide from 2012 to 2020 (in minutes), *Statista*, https://www. statista.com/statistics/433871/daily-social-media-usage-worldwide/# (archived at https://perma.cc/WTF7-QNBG)

SWEOR (2021) 27 eye-opening website statistics: is your website costing you clients? *SWEOR*, https://www.sweor.com/firstimpressions (archived at https://perma.cc/JB5Q-QDK6)

Chapter 5

DataReportal (2021) Global digital review, *DataReportal*, https:// datareportal.com/global-digital-overview (archived at https://perma. cc/8CGZ-PGFM)

Freeland Fisher, J (2020) How to get a job often comes down to one elite personal asset, and many people still don't realize it, CNBC, 14 February, https://www.cnbc.com/2019/12/27/how-to-get-a-job-often-comes-down-to-one-elite-personal-asset.html (archived at https:// perma.cc/2D62-BLEJ)

Groth, A (2012) You're the average of the five people you spend the most time with, *Insider,* 24 July, https://www.businessinsider.com/jim-rohn-youre-the-average-of-the-five-people-you-spend-the-most-time-with-2012-7?r=US&IR=T (archived at https://perma.cc/22KN-LHC7)

Oyserman, D (2015) Values, psychology of, in *International Encyclopedia of the Social & Behavioral Sciences*, 2nd edn, ed J D Wright, Elsevier, London

Chapter 6

Gov.uk (nd) Flexible working, GOV.UK, https://www.gov.uk/flexible-working/types-of-flexible-working (archived at https://perma.cc/ R2T3-J86R)

Gov.uk (2021) How to take on an apprentice, GOV.UK, https://www.gov.
uk/guidance/how-to-take-on-an-apprentice (archived at https://perma.
cc/7MNH-Z6TG)

Hunt, V *et al* (2018) Delivering through diversity, McKinsey & Company,
January, pp 1–2, https://www.mckinsey.com/~/media/mckinsey/
business%20functions/organization/our%20insights/delivering%20
through%20diversity/delivering-through-diversity_full-report.ashx
(archived at https://perma.cc/5Z4E-S46B)

Khan, S and Barlow, S (2021) Introduction to diversity & inclusion,
LinkedIn, 18 February, https://www.linkedin.com/posts/like-minded-
females_lmfnetwork-diversityandinclusion-business-activity-
6768485692570902528-6xWu (archived at https://perma.cc/8LTS-
SSRR)

Lorenzo, R *et al* (2018) How diverse leadership teams boost innovation,
Boston Consulting Group, 23 January, https://www.bcg.com/en-us/
publications/2018/how-diverse-leadership-teams-boost-innovation
(archived at https://perma.cc/5DLG-5RRK)

McLaren, S (2019) 6 stats that will change the way you write job posts,
LinkedIn, 24 January, https://business.linkedin.com/talent-solutions/
blog/job-descriptions/2019/stats-that-will-change-the-way-you-write-
job-posts (archived at https://perma.cc/9CV5-XC4U)

Sherbin, L and Rashid, R (2017) Diversity doesn't stick without inclusion,
Harvard Business Review, 1 February, https://hbr.org/2017/02/diversity-
doesnt-stick-without-inclusion (archived at https://perma.cc/N6JZ-HXXE)

Chapter 7

Black, S *et al* (1999) *Global Explorers: The next generation of leaders*,
Routledge, London

DiSC (nd) History of DiSC®, DiSC profile, https://www.discprofile.com/
what-is-disc/history-of-disc (archived at https://perma.cc/ST8E-TCVP)

Kirkpatrick, S and Locke, E (1991) Leadership: do traits matter?
Academy of Management Executive, 5 (2), pp 48–60

Morgan, J (2020) 14 top CEOs share their definition of 'leadership',
what's yours? *Medium,* 14 August, https://medium.com/jacob-
morgan/14-top-ceos-share-their-definition-of-leadership-whats-yours-
2b89a58576a6 (archived at https://perma.cc/P85E-DKLZ)

ResearchGate (2017) Are leaders born leaders or they acquire leadership by time? *ResearchGate*, https://www.researchgate.net/post/Are-leaders-born-leaders-or-they-acquire-leadership-by-time (archived at https://perma.cc/BRQ8-QRAV)

Sakulku, J and Alexander, J (2011) The impostor phenomenon, *International Journal of Behavioral Science*, 6 (1), pp 75–97

Templar (2021) Imposter syndrome-how it can help your career, Templar Advisors, https://templaradvisors.com/blog/impostor-syndrome-can-help-your-career (archived at https://perma.cc/6LD4-UN3A)

Chapter 8

Bannon, M T (2020) Startup founder mental health: why it matters and how to boost it, *Forbes*, 10 February, https://www.forbes.com/sites/marenbannon/2020/02/10/startup-founder-mental-health-why-it-matters-and-how-to-boost-it/?sh=4cfc5f5d1bf1 (archived at https://perma.cc/FD28-TLFK)

Bruder, J (2013) The psychological price of entrepreneurship, *Inc*, September, https://www.inc.com/magazine/201309/jessica-bruder/psychological-price-of-entrepreneurship.html (archived at https://perma.cc/B6EV-VSKQ)

Gevelber, L (2013) The shift to constant connectivity, *Think with Google*, May, https://www.thinkwithgoogle.com/marketing-strategies/search/shift-to-constant-connectivity/ (archived at https://perma.cc/HN7D-56WF)

Harvard Health (2019) Blueberries may help lower blood pressure, Harvard Health Publishing, 1 June, https://www.health.harvard.edu/staying-healthy/blueberries-may-help-lower-blood-pressure (archived at https://perma.cc/YR8H-R3PV)

McLeod, S (2006) Maslow's hierarchy of needs, *Simply Psychology*, https://www.simplypsychology.org/maslow.html (archived at https://perma.cc/66PR-P4SC)

Mind (2020) Mental health facts and statistics, Mind, https://www.mind.org.uk/information-support/types-of-mental-health-problems/statistics-and-facts-about-mental-health/how-common-are-mental-health-problems/ (archived at https://perma.cc/8GQJ-6RU3)

Saporito, T J (2012) It's time to acknowledge CEO loneliness, *Harvard Business Review*, 15 February, https://hbr.org/2012/02/its-time-to-acknowledge-ceo-lo (archived at https://perma.cc/QN4T-HT4X)

Chapter 9

Flint, M (2020) Cash flow: the reason 82% of small businesses fail, *Preferred CFO*, 8 June, https://www.preferredcfo.com/cash-flow-reason-small-businesses-fail/ (archived at https://perma.cc/K7ZJ-6SEB)

Warren, E and Tyagi, A (2006) *All Your Worth: The ultimate lifetime money plan*, Free Press, New York, NY

Chapter 10

Content Marketing Institute (2020). B2B Content Marketing 2020, Content Marketing Institute, https://contentmarketinginstitute.com/wp-content/uploads/2019/10/2020_B2B_Research_Final.pdf (archived at https://perma.cc/QD29-VNSQ)

Tam, J (nd) How to build a great series A pitch and deck, Y *Combinator*, https://www.ycombinator.com/library/8d-how-to-build-a-great-series-a-pitch-and-deck (archived at https://perma.cc/7MDM-2VTE)

Vuvoka, C (2021) 73+ surprising networking statistics to boost your career, *Review 42*, 26 February, https://review42.com/resources/networking-statistics/ (archived at https://perma.cc/9PJ5-AK3W)

Chapter 11

Leal, C J (2020) Getting stuff done with productive procrastination and Kanban, *Kanban Zone*, 8 September, https://kanbanzone.com/2020/getting-stuff-done-through-productive-procrastination-and-kanban/ (archived at https://perma.cc/4NFX-X4A6)

Index

CPSIA information can be obtained
at www.ICGtesting.com
Printed in the USA
JSHW040941091021
19419JS00007B/12